NATIONAL UNIVE~
LIBRARY   SAN D~

D0565274

Substitute
CIRCULATING
Teacher
Handb🍎k

Proven Professional
Management Skills &
Teaching Strategies

© **Substitute Teaching Institute**
Utah State University
6516 Old Main Hill
Logan, UT 84322-6516
(435) 797-3182
(800) 922-4693
SubEd@cc.usu.edu
http://subed.usu.edu
ISBN# 1-890563-11-0

FIFTH EDITION
Elementary K-8

NATIONAL UNIVERSITY
LIBRARY SAN DIEGO

NON CIRCULATING

NATIONAL UNIVERSITY
LIBRARY SAN DIEGO

What It's All About

Preface

Congratulations! You've decided to become a substitute teacher. Substitute teaching is an important educational component in our schools. It is a rare teacher who never needs a substitute for either personal or professional reasons. Principals, teachers, parents, and students value a good substitute teacher. Research has shown that a student spends over one full year with a substitute teacher by the time they graduate from high school. Skilled substitute teachers can have a significant, positive impact on the quality of education while the permanent teacher is away.

Regardless of whether or not you are a certified teacher, you can still become an expert in substitute teaching. Successful teachers are those who have either consciously, or subconsciously, developed the skills that make them effective in the classroom. In other words, by learning certain skills, techniques, and methods you can be a successful teacher. With these skills in your repertoire, you will be in such demand that you will be scheduling your substitute teaching assignments weeks in advance, students will see you in the hall and ask when you are coming to their class, and parents will be calling the district requesting they hire you full-time.

For information on Substitute Skills visit:

http:// subed.usu.edu

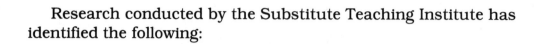

Research conducted by the Substitute Teaching Institute has identified the following:

■ *The number one request by permanent teachers and district personnel is that substitute teachers be prepared and professional.*

■ *The number one request by substitute teachers is the skill training to handle 94% of all classroom/behavior situations.*

■ *The number one request by students is that substitutes present stimulating lessons and exciting fill-in activities.*

■ *The number one trait of a successful substitute teacher is the use of a Super SubPack or resource kit.*

The contents of this book present these as well as other skills and strategies. Considerable time has been devoted to researching, documenting, and field-testing the ideas presented. Most of the theory behind these skills and strategies has been intentionally left out, in order to narrow the content to specific "do's" and "don'ts" of substitute teaching. The implementation of these skills and strategies will be one of the keys to your success as a substitute teacher.

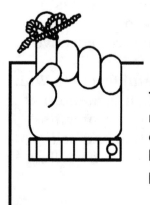

Remember

The information in this handbook is not intended to replace the rules and regulations of the district. Use only those suggestions and activities from this handbook that do not conflict with the district's policies.

Using This Book

This handbook is designed to give you, the substitute teacher, techniques, skills, and material to be more effective as you teach.

The icons (pictures) throughout the book are used to give visual recognition to tips, activities, and chapters. These icons will enable you to quickly locate each section and better understand what you are reading.

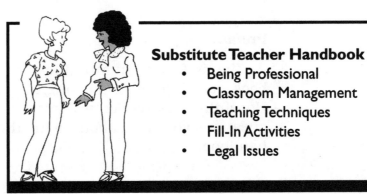

Substitute Teacher Handbook
- Being Professional
- Classroom Management
- Teaching Techniques
- Fill-In Activities
- Legal Issues

One Professional to Another

This icon presents key points in the section you are reading. By reviewing each box, you can quickly identify topics covered in the chapter.

Points to Ponder

This icon indicates key points to ponder or additional background information for the section you are reading.

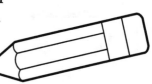

Remember

The remember icon points out important items or ideas you need to remember or take into consideration.

Super SubPack

The most common trait of successful substitute teachers is their possession of a "*bag of tricks*" that they bring to each assignment. During your study of this handbook, put together your own pack, bag, or resource kit to use in your classes. Suggested contents for a ***Super SubPack*** are listed on page 70.

Preface

The preface is an introduction to this book, its purpose, and contents. Hopefully, this section will answer questions you have about using the handbook.

Chapter 1: Being a Professional

Permanent teachers and district personnel unanimously request that substitute teachers be professional. Chapter One outlines aspects of being a professional substitute teacher, beginning well before the bell rings.

- At home
- Prior to entering the classroom
- In the classroom before school
- Throughout the day
- At the end of the day

Chapter 2: Classroom Management

No learning takes place in classrooms that are out-of-control. Chapter Two deals with managing the classroom learning environment. It contains ideas for starting the day, setting the tone, behavior management skills, and suggestions for managing challenging classroom scenarios.

Chapter 3: Other Stuff You Should Know

The other stuff you should know about includes:

- Safe Schools and Emergency Procedures
- First Aid
- Legal Aspects of the Job
- Disabilities and Special Education
- Gifted and Talented
- Multiculturism
- Alternative Learning
- Out of Classroom Activities

The information in this chapter should only be used to supplement local district policies and procedures.

Chapter 4: Teaching Strategies, Skills, and Suggestions

Chapter Four contains suggestions for the contents of your **Super SubPack**, methods for presenting the permanent teacher's lesson plans, and ideas for low cost/no cost rewards and motivators.

- Brainstorming
- Concept Mapping
- KWL
- Questions for Higher Level Thinking
- Cooperative Learning
- Using Audio Visual Materials Effectively

Chapter 5: Fill-In Activities

This chapter will give you many lesson and activity ideas for your **Super SubPack**. These "*fill-in*" activities can provide hours and hours of meaningful learning. A detailed *Table of Contents* listing individual activities is found in Chapter Five on pages 112 and 113. According to the type of activity, this chapter has been divided into three sections:

5-Minute Fillers

 Isn't it time to go yet?

Whole-class critical thinking activities for those extra five minutes that occur throughout the day.

Early Finishers

Independent activities for students who finish assignments early.

Short Activities

Teacher-directed activities and lessons. This section is organized by subject and includes lessons that can be taught in an hour or less.

- Art
- Critical Thinking
- Language Arts
- Math
- Science
- Adaptable (can be used for various subjects)

Overview Icon outlines the subject, grade level, materials needed, advance preparation required, and objective for each activity or lesson.

Notes For The Teacher:

These are found at the end of each *Short Activity* to point out classroom management techniques and background information specific to that lesson.

Contributing Authors

Geoffrey G. Smith

Mr. Smith is the Director of the Substitute Teaching Institute (STI) at Utah State University (USU), the principal investigator for STEP-IN (Substitute Teacher Educational Program Initiative), and has been the principal investigator for many substitute teacher projects. He is the publisher of the Substitute Teacher Handbooks, SubJournal and the *SubExchange* newsletter. He holds an MBA degree, a Masters in Educational Economics and has been involved with teacher-professional development for a number of years.

Cynthia Murdock

Ms. Murdock is the Curriculum Development Director at STI. Her teacher-leader ability, along with experience as a substitute and permanent teacher, provides a plethora of ideas and materials for substitute teachers. She has written and edited the *SubExchange* newsletter, several Substitute Teacher Handbooks and is also a teacher-professional development instructor.

Max L. Longhurst

Mr. Longhurst is the Elementary Education Specialist at STI/USU. He develops materials for substitute teachers, writes, field-tests, and conducts seminars and training sessions for educators. Having been in the classroom both as a permanent teacher and a substitute his experience provides practical applications for teaching and learning strategies.

Barbara Goldenhersh

Dr. Goldenhersh serves as an Assistant Professor of Education at Harris-Stowe State College, in St. Louis, MO. Along with teaching, she consults and presents nationally on topics including being an effective substitute teacher and school law. Books authored by Dr. Goldenhersh include, *The Guest Teacher: Being An Effective Substitute Teacher* and *Read It With Bookmarks*.

Glenn Latham

Dr. Latham is a Professor Emeritus of Special Education at USU and serves as a principal investigator at the Mountain Plains Regional Resource Center, which provides technical assistance for working with hard-to-teach and hard-to-manage students. Dr. Latham has also served as a consultant and advisor to numerous schools and school systems, both nationally and internationally. His publications include over 200 technical papers and journal articles as well as the book, *The Power of Positive Parenting: A Wonderful Way to Raise Children*.

A special thanks to: Chantry Brewer, Michelle Ditlevsen, Barbara Haines, Betty Hansen, Amber Hawkins, Shari Hobbs, Kevin Jones, Blaine Sorenson, Rosemary Weiland.

Table of Contents

The Professional Substitute Teacher

Chapter 1

Introduction

Through thousands of surveys, questionnaires, and interviews, we have learned that permanent teachers, school administrators, and district personnel unanimously praise and value substitute teachers who are professional in dress, attitude, and presentation.

Being a professional substitute teacher is an all-day job. It involves many aspects of attitude and conduct. In this chapter, these aspects have been organized into the following five time frames:

1. At Home
2. Prior to Entering the Classroom
3. In the Classroom Before School
4. Throughout the Day
5. At the End of the Day

For additional information regarding the Professional Substitute Teacher, visit:

http://subed.usu.edu

The Professional Substitute Teacher

At Home

There are a number of things you can do at home before you ever get that early morning call to substitute teach.

- Prepare a set of note cards, one for each school where you may be called to teach. On each card, list the name of the school, principal, and secretary, school phone numbers, start time, address, driving directions, and the approximate time it will take to travel from your home to this location.

- Place a notebook and pencil by the phone you will be using to answer early morning calls. You may even want to jot down a couple of pertinent questions to ask when the call comes such as, *"What is the name and grade level of the teacher I will be substituting for?"*

- Assemble a **Super Sub Pack** filled with teaching supplies and activity ideas for the grade levels you teach. (For more information about **Super Sub Packs**, see page 70.)

- Designate a section of your closet for substitute teaching clothes. Assemble entire outfits, including shoes and socks, which are ironed and ready to be put on at a moment's notice. Be sure to select comfortable shoes, since as an effective substitute you will be on your feet all day. Have several different outfits ready so that you are prepared to dress appropriately for different grade levels and subject assignments.

- Research has shown that teachers who dress professionally command more respect in the classroom than those who dress casually or inappropriately. Gain the respect you deserve by the way you dress.

Appropriate Attire Guidelines for Men and Women

Women: Avoid high heels, short skirts, and low-cut tops. Select comfortable outfits in which you can bend down, stoop over, and write on chalkboards with ease.

Men: Consider wearing a tie with a button-down shirt. You can always take off the tie, undo the neck button, and roll up your sleeves if you find yourself "over-dressed" for the assignment.

As a general rule, jeans, t-shirts, sandals, and other casual clothing are not considered professional nor appropriate for the classroom setting. You should always dress at least as professionally as your permanent teacher counterparts.

When the call comes, answer the phone yourself. A groggy spouse or roommate does not always make a professional impression, and you will be wasting the caller's time while they are waiting for you to wake up and get to the phone.

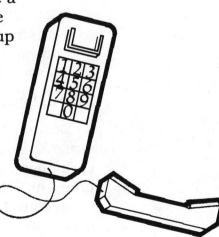

After you hang the phone, take a look at your note card for the school, determine how long it will take you to get there, and plan the rest of the morning accordingly. Remember that you want to be at the school at least 20 minutes prior to the beginning of class, or prior to when students arrive. Get ready and don't forget to grab your **Super Sub Pack** as you head out the door.

Prior to Entering the Classroom

Enter the school enthusiastic and serious about your role. If possible, arrive at least 20 minutes prior to the beginning of class. Report to the principal or office to let them know you have arrived, and ask pertinent questions:

Will I be responsible for playground, lunch, or bus duty?

Do any of the students have medical problems I should be aware of?

If the need arises, how do I refer a student to the office?

How do I report students who are tardy or absent?

Obtain any keys that might be necessary.

Find the locations of restrooms, the teacher's lounge, the cafeteria, the auditorium, the media center, and the nearest drinking fountain before school begins.

Meet neighboring teachers.

In the Classroom Before School

Enter the classroom with confidence, and your **Super SubPack**. Put your name on the board, then familiarize yourself with the room. Locate and review the classroom rules and evacuation map.

Read through lesson plans left by the permanent teacher and identify books, handouts, and papers that will be needed throughout the day. Study the classroom seating chart. If you can't find a seating chart, get ready to make your own (see page 17).

When the bell rings, stand in the doorway and greet students as they enter the classroom. Be professional, friendly, and enthusiastic about the day. This first impression will take you a long way.

Throughout the Day

Do your best to follow the lesson plans and carry out the assigned duties left by the permanent teacher. Over 75% of permanent teachers report that they spend at least 45 minutes preparing lesson plans and materials for substitute teachers. Having invested both time and energy into these plans, permanent teachers feel very strongly about having them carried out.

On the other hand, you may enter a classroom where you are unable to locate the lesson plans or necessary materials. In

such a case, act quickly, calmly, and confidently. By utilizing materials and ideas in your Super SubPack, you can still have a productive day.

Whatever situation or challenge you are faced with, always strive to be positive and respectful. Permanent teachers care about the students in their class. They know each student's strengths and weaknesses, and will want to see those areas handled appropriately. They hope the substitute teacher will appreciate the good in their students and bring out the best in them.

Permanent teachers urge substitute teachers to be aware of how small things, like using a normal voice, giving praise, and having an upbeat attitude can affect students. Students resent teachers who talk down to them, make promises or threats they don't intend to keep, and are not fair in administering rewards and consequences. Treating students as individuals is important. Don't blame the whole class nor punish the group for the misdeeds of a few. (See Chapter Two for suggestions on classroom management.)

When a substitute teacher uses good judgment, avoids criticism, and adapts to circumstances in a positive way, the teacher becomes a professional role model for both the students in the class and other teachers.

At the End of the Day

Being a professional is just as important at the end of the day as it is at the beginning. What you do just before the final bell will be the impression students take home with them. How you leave the classroom will be the first impression a permanent teacher has of you when they return.

Before the Students Leave

There are several things you should do during the last few minutes of class before the students leave:

- If the teacher has classroom sets (calculators, scissors, books, etc.), be sure to have them all returned before the students leave the room. It is much easier to locate a missing calculator in a class of 30, than trying to find it somewhere in the whole school.

- Challenge students to recall, and list on the board, projects and topics they have studied that day. *(Now they will have a positive answer when parents ask what they did in school, instead of the traditional, "Nothing", we had a Sub.")*

- Remind students of homework. Writing homework assignments on the board throughout the day will help both you and the students remember.

- Have students straighten and clean-up the area around their desk.

After the Students Have Left

After the students have gone, take a few minutes to complete your professional duties as a substitute teacher. Fill out a "Substitute Teacher Report" for the permanent teacher (see sample form on the following page). Write a detailed summary of what was accomplished throughout the day, along with any problems that arose and notes about things that went well, or students that were particularly helpful.

If, for any reason, you were unable to carry out the plans left by the permanent teacher, be sure to explain why you were unable to carry them out and what you did instead. Leave your name, phone number, and an invitation for the permanent teacher to contact you if they have any questions, or to request you as their substitute again in the future.

Leave the teacher's desk and assignments turned in by students neatly organized. Close windows, turn off lights and equipment, and double check to make sure the room is in good order before you lock the door and head for the office. At the office, return keys, turn in any money collected, express appreciation for assistance provided, and check to see if you will be needed again the next day.

In Conclusion

Teachers have high expectations of others who come into their classroom. By implementing the ideas in this chapter, you can become a professional that meets and exceeds these expectations. Always remember that you are a valued and important part of the educational system. Never diminish your role as a substitute teacher. Teachers appreciate having a person come into their classroom who is caring and capable. By being prepared, poised, and professional, you will greatly reduce the stress on the teacher, students, and yourself. The checklist on pages 8 and 9 will help you stay on the right track throughout the day. Additional hints and suggestions are found at the end of Chapter Four, on page 104.

Substitute Teacher Report

Substitute: _____   Date: _____

Phone Number: _____   Grade: _____

Substituted for: _____   School: _____

Notes regarding lesson plans:

I also taught:

Notes regarding behavior:

Terrific helpers:

Students who were absent:

Messages for the permanent teacher:

Please let me know of any areas you feel I can improve, to be a better substitute for you.

© Substitute Teaching Institute/Utah State University

☑ Professional Substitute Teacher Checklist

At Home

_____ Compile a set of note cards containing pertinent information about the schools where you may be assigned.

_____ Keep a notebook and pen by the phone you use to answer early morning calls.

_____ Assemble a **Super SubPack.** Keep it well stocked and ready.

_____ Organize several appropriate substitute teacher outfits in a section of your closet.

_____ Answer the phone yourself.

_____ Leave early enough to arrive at school at least 20 minutes prior to the beginning of school.

Prior to Entering the Classroom

_____ Report to the principal or the office.

_____ Ask about student passes, playground rules, bus duty, and lunch procedures.

_____ Ask if there will be any special duties associated with the permanent teacher's assignment.

_____ Find out how to refer a student to the office.

_____ Ask if any children have medical problems.

_____ Obtain necessary keys.

_____ Ask how to report students who are tardy or absent.

_____ Find the locations of restrooms, the teachers' lounge, and other important places in the school.

_____ Introduce yourself to the teachers on both sides of your classroom.

In the Classroom Before School

_____ Enter the classroom with confidence and your **Super SubPack**.

_____ Put your name on the board.

_____ Review the classroom rules.

_____ Locate and review the school evacuation map.

_____ Read through the lesson plans left by the permanent teacher.

_____ Locate books, papers, and materials which will be needed throughout the day.

_____ Study the seating chart and if you can't find one get ready to make your own.

_____ When the bell rings, stand in the doorway and greet students as they enter the classroom.

Throughout the Day

_____ Greet students at the door and get them involved in learning activities quickly.

_____ Carry out the lesson plans and assigned duties to the best of your ability.

_____ Improvise using the materials in your **Super SubPack** to fill extra time, enhance activities, or supplement sketchy lesson plans as needed.

_____ Be fair and carry out the rewards and consequences you establish.

_____ Be positive and respectful in your interactions with students and school personnel.

At the End of the Day

_____ Make sure all classroom sets are accounted for.

_____ Challenge students to recall projects and topics they have studied that day.

_____ Remind students of homework.

_____ Have students straighten and clean the area around their desks.

_____ Complete a "Substitute Teacher Report" for the permanent teacher.

_____ Neatly organize papers turned in by students.

_____ Close windows, turn off lights and equipment, and make sure the room is in good order, before you lock the door.

_____ Turn in keys and any money collected at the office.

_____ Thank individuals who provided assistance during the day.

_____ Check to see if you will be needed again the next day.

Classroom Management

Chapter 2

Effective
Classroom & Behavior Management

This chapter explains five behavior management skills and various strategies to help you effectively manage student behavior and the classroom environment. The skills presented have been developed by Dr. Glenn Latham* and, when implemented correctly, have been statistically proven to prevent/eliminate 94% of inappropriate student behavior.

As you come to understand and implement these skills and strategies, your ability to effectively manage the classroom environment (use of time, organization of events, etc.) and direct student behavior will increase. Unfortunately, there isn't one "true" recipe that guarantees appropriate student behavior or a successful day in the classroom, but these guiding principles and skills have been proven successful in making the most of any situation.

* Dr. Latham is the principal investigator for the Mountain Plains Regional Resource Center at Utah State University.

To adapt more skills as a Professional Substitute Teacher, visit:

http:// subed.usu.edu

Behavior Management

A Brief Note About Principles of Human Behavior

Behavior is largely a product of its immediate environment.

Behavior is largely a product of its immediate environment.

If students misbehave, act out, are easily distracted, and so on, it is very likely that this is in response to something in the immediate classroom environment. To a large degree, your actions as a teacher determine this environment.

Behavior is strengthened or weakened by its consequences.

The persistent behavior of students who are disruptive or non-attentive can invariably be explained by the classroom consequences of this behavior.

Behavior ultimately responds better to positive than to negative consequences.

By genuinely reinforcing appropriate behavior through positive consequences, many undesirable behaviors will become extinct and appropriate behavior among all students will increase.

Whether a behavior has been punished or reinforced is known only by the course of that behavior in the future.

The only way you can tell if a response to a behavior is punishing or reinforcing is to watch what happens to the behavior after the response. What is a punishment to one student may reinforce and perpetuate a behavior in another.

Five Skills for Effective Behavior Management
- Teaching expectations
- Getting and keeping students on-task
- Positive teacher-to-pupil interactions and risk-free student response opportunities
- Responding noncoercively
- Avoiding being trapped

Five Skills for Effective Behavior Management

The following skills for managing student behavior are based on these basic principles of human behavior. Understanding and effectively implementing these skills will help prevent unnecessary classroom management problems, as well as prepare you to manage any challenging situations which may occur.

Skill #1   The ability to teach expectations.

Skill #2   The ability to get and keep students on-task.

Skill #3   The ability to maintain a high rate of positive teacher-to-pupil interactions and risk-free student response opportunities.

Skill #4   The ability to respond noncoercively.

Skill #5   The ability to avoid being trapped.

Skill #1: The ability to teach expectations.

Teaching expectations involves communicating to students the behaviors that are expected in the classroom. Types of expectations include:

1. Classroom expectations (rules)
2. Instructional expectations
3. Procedural expectations

Expectations should provide boundaries and establish standards for student success.

As a substitute teacher, your first objective should be to model the expectations of the permanent teacher. Locate the classroom rules posted in the classroom and try to determine the procedures and strategies used by the permanent teacher to get the attention of the class. This can be accomplished by reviewing the lesson plans and talking to students. If there are no rules or procedures in evidence, be prepared to implement your own.

Classroom expectations should be concise, specific, instructive, operational, and must convey an expectation of student behavior. Phrases such as "*be cooperative*," "*respect others*," and "*be polite and helpful*" are too general and take too much time to explain. Effective expectations such as, "*Follow

Rules:
General standards of behavior that are expected throughout the day (i.e., use appropriate language at all times).

Instructions:
Information about what students are supposed to do (i.e., complete the crossword puzzle).

Procedures: The manner and methods students use to follow instructions and comply with rules (i.e., read silently).

directions the first time they are given," are direct, provide specific standards, and are appropriate for any grade level. The number of expectations should correlate with the age and ability of the students; in general, it is recommended they be limited to five or less.

Once general classroom behavior expectations have been taught, they should be posted somewhere in the room. Hopefully, the permanent teacher has already done this. If not, you can post them on the board or on a poster-size sheet of paper you carry in your *Super SubPack.* In primary grades, using pictures in addition to words is a good way to convey your expectations.

Each assignment and activity throughout the day will have its own set of instructional and procedural expectations. *Instructional expectations* and *Procedural expectations* need to be communicated to students in order for students to successfully complete their assignments.

As you develop and explain instructional and procedural expectations, realize that students need three things in order to successfully meet the expectations you establish:

1. They need to know exactly what it is they are supposed to do.
   Example: Finish your math assignment.

2. They need to know how they are expected to do it.
   Example: Work with your partner and raise your hand if you need help.

3. They need to have the necessary tools to accomplish the expected task.
   Examples: Paper, pencil, calculator, etc.

Examples of Instruction Expectations:

- Pass your worksheet to the front of the row.
- Number your paper from 1 to 10.
- Write a 500 word essay.
- Read the story.

Examples of Procedure Expectations:

- Work silently.
- Keep all your materials on the desk.
- Walk in a single file line.
- Talk with group members using a quiet voice.

Sample Classroom Expectations (Rules)

- Follow directions the first time they are given.
- Raise your hand for permission to speak.
- Keep hands, feet, and objects to yourself.
- Always walk in the classroom and halls.
- Use language that builds others.
- Complete assignments in the allotted time.
- Perform your tasks during group activities.
- Do your best work.
- Use appropriate language.

Explaining instructional and procedural expectations in the form of a step-by-step process often makes it easier for students to remember the expectations and complete the corresponding task appropriately.

Step-By-Step Strategy

◀ Strategy

One reoccurring teaching situation where it is especially important to designate specific expectations is when students are making the transition from one activity to another. Students often waste time between activities because seemingly simple instructions such as, "*Get ready for math*," are in reality quite ambiguous. Students need to know the following five specific things to make a quick transition from one activity to the next:

1. How to close their engagement in the current activity.

2. What to do with the materials they are using.

3. What new materials they will need.

4. What to do with these new materials.

5. How much time they have to make the transition.

Example: "*Stop reading and quietly put your reading book away. Get out your math book and paper. Open the book to page 112. You have one minute to do this. Please begin.*"

Just telling students what your expectations are is often not enough. Expectations should be explained, restated by the students, demonstrated, and role-played until you are sure the students understand what is expected of them. Questioning students can help determine if this has been accomplished. Having students respond as an entire group and act out behaviors, such as raising their hand, is also a good idea as it requires every student in the class to understand and acknowledge the expectation.

Have Students Restate Expectations

Having students restate expectations is one way to ensure that they understand/acknowledge the expectations.

Teacher: (Calling on an attentive student) "*Robbie, thank you for paying attention. What do I expect you to do when you want to answer a question or say something?*"

Robbie: "*You want me to raise my hand.*"

Teacher: "*That's right, Robbie. I expect you to raise your hand.*"

The few minutes it takes to communicate expectations for each activity are well worth the stress and inappropriate behavior that will be prevented. Once you have established your expectations, stick with them! Students will remember what you have said and expect you to follow through. Firmness, fairness, and consistency are the keys to classroom management. Praising students when expectations are met will reinforce and perpetuate appropriate student behavior.

Skill #2: The ability to get and keep students on-task.

It doesn't take a rocket scientist to figure out that students cannot learn if they are not actively engaged in learning activities. To be actively engaged in an assigned activity is commonly referred to as being "on-task." When students are on-task, they will learn more and create fewer classroom management problems. Getting and keeping students on-task can usually be accomplished using two simple strategies:

1. Begin instruction/activities immediately.

2. Manage by walking around.

Begin Instruction/Activities Immediately

The shorter the time between the beginning of class and when students are actively involved in a productive activity the better. Begin the day by introducing yourself and immediately engaging students in a structured activity. Some permanent teachers may leave instructions for a "self-starter" activity which students routinely complete at the beginning of class. If such an activity is not outlined in the lesson plans, implement an activity of your own. Many effective substitute teachers start the day by having students make name tags, help construct a seating chart, or participate in one of the Five-Minute Filler activities found in Chapter Five.

Introductory activities serve two purposes in the classroom. First, they get students actively engaged in a learning activity and thereby decrease the opportunity for inappropriate behavior. Second, they provide a means for you as the substitute teacher to assess the personality of the class. This assessment can help you as you begin implementing the lesson plans left by the permanent teacher.

Name Tags

Name tags can be worn or kept on student desks throughout the day. They can be made using commercial stick-on name tags, adhesive file folder labels, or strips of masking tape. Name

Begin Class Immediately

"Hello. My name is ... and I am your teacher today. Please spend the next five minutes completing the activity I have outlined on the board."

Starting the Day

- Greet students at the door.
- Introduce yourself as the teacher.
- Get students doing something.
- Name Tags and Seating Chart.
- Establish a plan for the day.

tags are a tremendous help when facilitating class discussions and managing student behavior.

Seating Chart

A seating chart is a valuable tool that you can use throughout the day to take roll, and assist you in calling students by name. However, sometimes you may not be able to locate a seating chart, or the seating chart left by the permanent teacher may not be current. If this is the case, it is easy for you to quickly make a seating chart using small Post-it Notes® and a file folder from your *Super SubPack*. Distribute one Post-it Note® to each student and have them write their name on it. After students have done this, arrange the names on the file folder in the same configuration as the desks in the classroom (see example below). The few minutes it takes to establish an accurate seating chart at the beginning of class is well worth the benefits it will provide.

After an introductory activity, try to minimize the time spent on procedural matters such as taking roll and lunch count. Dragging these activities out simply provides time for students to get bored and start behaving inappropriately. After taking roll and attending to any other beginning of class matters, outline for students your plan and schedule of activities for the day. Now is the time to quickly review expectations, explain

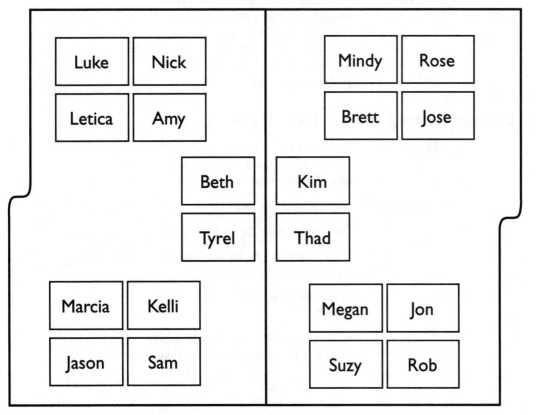

consequences of student behavior, and introduce any incentives or special activities you will be using. Share with students information left by the permanent teacher regarding what they should accomplish during the day, then get students involved in the next learning activity as quickly as possible.

The sooner you get students on-task, the easier it is to keep them actively engaged in constructive activities. Do not allow yourself to get drawn off-task by student protests and long useless discussions. If students complain, respond with empathy, understanding, and firmness, but don't compromise your expectations or waste instructional time being overly sympathetic.

Students Getting the Teacher Off-Task

Teacher:	*"Please take out your reading books and read silently at your desk for the next 20 minutes."*
Students:	*"Reading is boring."*
	"We never read before lunch."
	"Our teacher lets us sit anywhere in the room when we read."
	"Twenty minutes is too long of a time."
Teacher:	*"You know when I was your age, I thought reading was boring too. Sometimes I used to just sit at my desk, hold my book open, and pretend to read. Have any of you ever done anything like that?"*

Teacher Getting the Students On-Task

Don't let students draw you off-task.

Teacher:	*"Please take out your reading books and read silently at your desk for the next 20 minutes."*
Students:	*"Reading is boring."*
	"We never read before lunch."
	"Our teacher lets us sit anywhere in the room when we read."
	"Twenty minutes is too long of a time."
Teacher:	*"I understand that silent reading may not be your favorite activity and*

this may not be the way Mrs. Jones does it, however, today we are going to read silently, at our desks, for the next 20 minutes. Please take out your reading books and begin."

Manage by Walking Around

Respond to protests with empathy, firmness, and fairness.

The easiest and most effective strategy for keeping student on-task is for the teacher to walk around the classroom in a random pattern. By moving about the room, you can observe the progress of students, acknowledge and reinforce positive behavior, and manage off-task behavior with proximity (nearness to the student). There is a direct relationship between how close a teacher is to students and how well students behave. Proximity is important! So wear comfortable shoes and plan to be on your feet all day monitoring, assisting, providing positive reinforcement, and using proximity to keep students on-task.

Other On-Task Strategies

In some circumstances, additional strategies are needed to get and keep students on-task. Sometimes an event outside the classroom, such as an assembly, fire drill, or rousing game of soccer at recess, will make it difficult to get and keep students on-task. On other occasions, the entire class may be off-task or out of control for no apparent reason at all. Often the permanent teacher may have strategies and techniques such as silent signals or prompt/response drills, which can be implemented to get the attention of, or refocus, the class. If such techniques have been outlined in the lesson plans or explained by a student, don't hesitate to implement them. If you are left to manage the situation on your own, implement appropriate, positive, and proactive strategies.

Refocusing the Class: Captivate and Redirect

Often the best way to deal with major disruptions such as assemblies and fire drills is to minimize the event by capturing and redirecting students' attention. For example, complete an activity that requires mental concentration such as a *5-Minute Filler* or *Critical Thinking Activity* from this book. You may also want to try the *Silent Lesson* found on page 232. Involving students in a fun and mentally challenging learning activity will help them settle down to the routine of the day.

Getting Their Attention Strategies: Whisper, Write & Erase, and Lights Out

On occasion the entire class may be off-task, in the middle of an assignment, or just finishing an activity when you need to get their attention in order to get everyone back on-task, give further instructions, or conclude the activity. The first thing you should do is try the strategy usually used by the permanent teacher such as a silent signal or prompt/response. If this is unsuccessful, or you don't know what the permanent teacher usually does, the following are three strategies that will get the attention of the entire class.

Strategy ▶

Whisper

Your first instinct in a situation where the entire class is noisy and off-task may be to raise your voice above the noise level of the room and demand attention. However, this can incur some unwelcome side effects, such as the students hearing you speak loudly and assuming it is OK for them to raise their voices as well. A productive strategy is to whisper. Move to the front of the room and begin giving instructions very quietly. As students hear you, they will need to become quiet in order to understand what you are saying. Soon students who are still talking and interacting will instinctively begin to feel uncomfortable and become silent also. When you have the attention of the entire class, you can then give instructions or directions as needed.

Strategy ▶

Write & Erase

If the class is between activities and talking among themselves, one way to get their attention and give further instructions is to begin writing and erasing the student instructions on the board one word at a time. For example, if you wanted them to get their Social Studies book out of their desk you would write the word "Get" on the chalkboard then erase it, then you would write the word "your" and erase it, then write the word "Social" and erase it, etc. Students will soon become so involved in trying to figure out what you are writing (and what words they missed) that you will very quickly have the undivided attention of the entire class.

Lights Out

This strategy should only be used when you need the attention of the entire class, and you will not be unnecessarily interrupting students who are on-task (i.e., students are busy working on group projects and you need everyone's attention to quickly give instructions for concluding the activity before lunch). Quickly turn the classroom lights off then on again. Be prepared to begin speaking in the moment of surprised silence, when you have everyone's undivided attention. If you wait too long to start talking, the class will begin talking about the lights going out and the event itself will become a real distraction.

Skill #3: The ability to maintain a high rate of positive teacher-to-pupil interactions and risk-free student response opportunities.

Positive Teacher-to-Pupil Interactions

Student behaviors are reinforced as they are recognized through teacher-to-pupil interactions. On average, educators allow 98% of all appropriate behavior to go unrecognized and are two to three times more likely to recognize inappropriate behavior. It has been shown that strengthening desirable behavior through positive reinforcement, rather than trying to weaken undesirable behavior using aversive or negative processes, will do more to make a classroom conducive to learning than any other single skill.

In general, positive verbal praise, a smile, a nod, and other appropriate gestures are among the very best ways to interact in a positive manner with students. Negative and corrective interactions should be outnumbered by positive interactions. A ratio of one negative to eight positive interactions is recommended. For ideas of positive things you can say to students, see the list of *101 Ways to Say Good Job,* on page 93.

To become more positive in challenging situations, you must identify and practice positive interaction skills. One way to do this is to determine situations in which you are most inclined to be negative, using a form such as this on page 22.

On the left side of the paper, describe a problem or inappropriate behavior that is most likely to elicit a negative response from you. On the right side of the paper, write a positive, proactive response(s) that could be used instead. Remember that you are learning a new skill, and need to practice several times in order to become proficient.

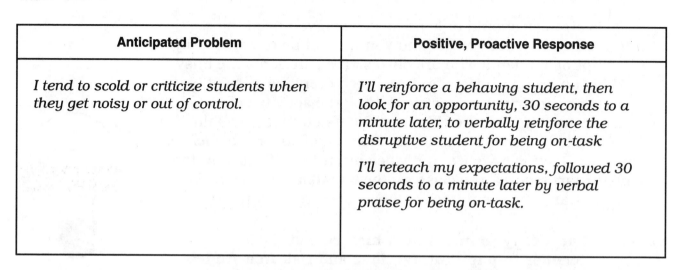

Anticipated Problem	Positive, Proactive Response
I tend to scold or criticize students when they get noisy or out of control.	*I'll reinforce a behaving student, then look for an opportunity, 30 seconds to a minute later, to verbally reinforce the disruptive student for being on-task* *I'll reteach my expectations, followed 30 seconds to a minute later by verbal praise for being on-task.*

At times, situations will arise that will be so annoying and unnerving that every positive interaction you have ever practiced will completely escape your recollection. When you can't think of an appropriate way to respond and are overwhelmed with the urge to react in a negative manner, **don't do anything**! Unless what you are about to say or do has a high probability for making things better, it is better to do nothing at all.

Strategy ▶

Positive Interaction Strategy: The Designated Problem Student

On occasion, a teacher may leave a note about a student to "watch out for," or a neighboring teacher may warn you about a "trouble maker." In such situations, you can often gain the compliance of the student and prevent potential problems by being proactive and positive. When the students arrive, determine who the identified student is and request that he or she be a "helper" for the day. Ask him or her to help you and provide special jobs that keep him/her positively occupied. Be positive in your interactions and thank them for their assistance. Provide the attention usually gained through negative behavior for acting as a helper. This strategy often defuses the problem before it ever becomes one and creates a "ringleader" for positive behavior.

Strategy ▶

Positive Interaction Strategy: The "You vs. Them" Class

Sometimes you may get the feeling that the whole class, or at least several of the students, have secretly planned to make the day as difficult as possible for you, the substitute teacher. Most "You vs. Them" scenarios turn out to be a lose-lose situation for everyone involved. Take the initiative early in the day to do a teacher and student interactive activity. You might try an activity from the *5-Minute Filler* section of this book, such as a Mystery Box, a Silly Story, or Number Phrase. Interact with the students, let them see that you have a sense of humor and get to know you better. Chances are, once you break the ice and establish a rapport with students the remainder of the day will go more smoothly. Making the classroom a battleground for control will usually make things worse.

Risk-Free Student Response Opportunities

◀ Strategy

Student response opportunities and active participation in the learning process play an important role in student achievement. As an added benefit, when students are engaged in appropriate responses to learning activities they have neither the inclination, nor the time, to be engaged in inappropriate behavior.

One aspect of providing risk-free student response opportunities is to provide response opportunities in the first place. Lecture little and question much. Let students answer questions that illustrate or explain the point you are trying to get across.

A second aspect of risk-free student response is to provide all students with opportunities and invitations to respond and inquire. There are always students with their hands raised continually, anxious to say just about anything. On the other hand, there are also those students who sit in class like a lump, never asking a question or making a comment. As a teacher, it is easy to get in the habit of calling on students who are attentive, interested, and willing to volunteer information. A simple way to insure that all students have a chance to respond, while at the same time maintaining the students' attention, is to place the names of all the students in a container and draw them out randomly. After a student has responded, put their name back in the container, otherwise they will lose interest and stop paying attention because they think they won't be called on again.

The third component of risk-free student response is to maintain a learning environment where students are not afraid to respond, an environment that is "risk-free" of failure and criticism. This can be accomplished by:

a) Asking the student to repeat what has been said.

b) Prompting the student in the direction of a correct response.

c) Asking students who you think know the answer.

d) Directing students' attention to a correct response.

Failure is a negative, ineffective, and poor teacher. In order to establish and maintain a risk-free classroom environment, do everything possible to help students have successful experiences. As you provide opportunities for students to give correct responses, you are also setting up opportunities to positively acknowledge these successes.

Handling Wrong Answers: Echo the Correct Response

Suppose you asked a student a question expecting a correct response but for whatever reason the student didn't give the right answer. In such situations, don't dwell on the failure of the student or the incorrectness of the answer. Instead, direct the question and the student's attention to another student who you are quite sure knows the answer. Once the question has been answered correctly, come back to the original student and ask the question again, allowing them to echo the correct response, and thus creating a successful experience for the student.

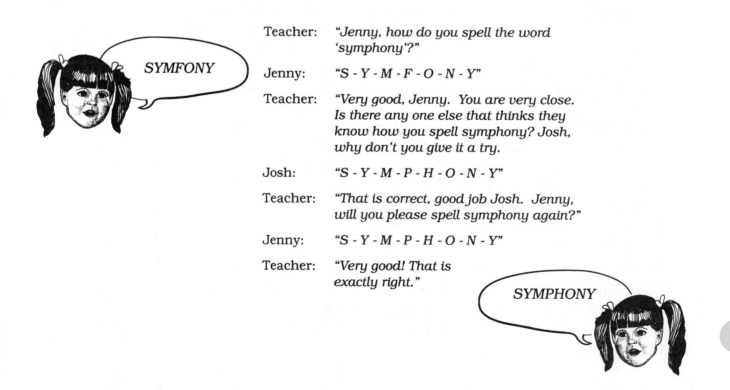

Teacher:	*"Jenny, how do you spell the word 'symphony'?"*
Jenny:	*"S - Y - M - F - O - N - Y"*
Teacher:	*"Very good, Jenny. You are very close. Is there any one else that thinks they know how you spell symphony? Josh, why don't you give it a try.*
Josh:	*"S - Y - M - P - H - O - N - Y"*
Teacher:	*"That is correct, good job Josh. Jenny, will you please spell symphony again?"*
Jenny:	*"S - Y - M - P - H - O - N - Y"*
Teacher:	*"Very good! That is exactly right."*

Occasionally, students will respond inaccurately, inappropriately, or even foolishly on purpose. Do not allow yourself to be drawn off target and into their control. Even though the student response was inappropriate, it is probably inconsequential. Overlook it and move forward with the instructional activity. Redirect the question to another student who you know is likely to respond correctly and appropriately, provide positive reinforcement for the correct response, then continue with the discussion. Responding to the inappropriate comment will most likely reinforce the behavior and prompt other students to engage in such responses.

Skill #4: The ability to respond noncoercively.

Any time a student behaves inappropriately you will probably find it annoying. However, the type of behavior, rather than the annoyance level, should be your guide for implementing an appropriate teacher response strategy. Inappropriate student behaviors can be classified as either consequential or inconsequential. Consequential behaviors are those which have a significant negative effect on the learning environment and interfere with the rights of other students to learn. Inconsequential behaviors are those which the classroom environment would be better off without, but their negative impact on student learning is minimal. Inconsequential behaviors, such as tapping a pencil on the desk, can become consequential if they escalate or persist over a period of time.

Ignore the Inconsequential

Ignore inconsequential behavior.

Most inappropriate student behavior, regardless of how annoying it is, is inconsequential. This means that it is not life threatening, it isn't going to destroy the building or its contents, nor does it indicate that a student is on the road to rack and ruin. A substitute teacher responding to inconsequential student behavior is providing reinforcement, and the frequency of these behaviors will likely increase. A better approach is to ignore inconsequential behavior and respond positively to appropriate behavior with a smile, verbal praise, or other appropriate gesture.

Example of Ignoring Inconsequential Behavior

When asking a question of the class, a student responds without raising their hand for permission to speak or speaks out-of-turn when a student response is not called for.

Step 1:   Do not respond to the disruptive student. Look positively at those who are raising their hand and call on one of them saying, *"Thank you for raising your hand,"* then allow them to answer the question.

Step 2:   If the student continues to speak without raising their hand when you ask the next question, continue to reinforce the students who are behaving appropriately and move closer to the student who is not cooperating.

Do not acknowledge the student who is speaking out of turn. If you give in and let that student answer, you will be reinforcing the inappropriate behavior. Generally after Steps 1 and 2, a noncompliant student will cooperate and the inappropriate behavior will have stopped. It is important to quickly recognize and reinforce the appropriate behavior of students as they stop behaving inappropriately and comply with expectations.

Respond Noncoercively to Consequential Behavior

Respond noncoercively to consequential behavior.

While most student behavior is inconsequential, there are inappropriate student behaviors that are of consequence and need to be addressed. Such behaviors would include those in which a student persists in disruptive behavior and is increasingly destroying the learning environment, or when students are physically or verbally abusive to one another. Coercion is a common inappropriate response to such behavior.

Coercion involves interactions with students that attempt to achieve compliance through the use of threats or force. The intent is to compel students to behave out of a fear of what will happen to them if they don't. Coercion makes a student want to escape or avoid their coercer, it does nothing to address the problem. At best, it will instill a sense of fear in students which prevents them from acting out. While on the surface the problem seems to have gone away, in reality you've threatened the student's self-confidence and destroyed the atmosphere of risk-free student response opportunities you are trying to create.

A better way to handle such situations is to stop, then redirect student behavior. This should be done as privately and quietly as possible. The following are six steps for stopping and redirecting inappropriate student behavior:

1. Say something positive.

2. Briefly describe the problem behavior.

3. Describe the desired alternative behavior.

4. Give a reason why the new behavior is more desirable.

5. Practice the desired behavior.

6. Provide positive feedback.

An example of how this would be done in the classroom setting:

1. Say something positive.	*"Beth, I enjoy having you in class. You have a lot of very creative ideas."*
2. Describe the problem behavior.	*"Just now when I asked you to stop tapping on your desk with your pencil and read silently, you continued to tap your pencil."*
3. Describe the desired behavior.	*"When I ask you to do something, you need to look at me, say OK or nod, and follow my instructions immediately."*
4. Reason the new behavior is desirable.	*"If you will stop tapping your pencil, the classroom will be quieter and everyone, including you, will be able to finish the reading assignment more quickly."*
5. Practice the desired behavior.	*"Beth, what are the three things you should do when I give you instructions?"* (Beth says, *"Look at you, say OK, and do it."*) If Beth does not respond, prompt her. If she responds inappropriately, repeat the question without displaying anger. Then say, *"Let's practice. I'll ask you to put your pencil down on the desk, and you show me the correct way to follow these instructions."*
6. Provide positive feedback.	*"Beth, you did a great job saying OK and putting down your pencil, but you forgot to look at me. Let's try it again, and this time remember to do all three steps."* (Beth responds correctly the second time.) The teacher says, *"Great! This time you looked at me, said OK, and put down your pencil. Good job!"*

Though this process may seem cumbersome and complicated, it actually takes less than two minutes and will become quite natural when practiced consistently. At this point, you might be thinking, "Well that's all right for young students, but not for the kids I work with." It may interest you to know that this strategy was developed at Boy's Town in Omaha, Nebraska, and is used daily with boys and girls of all ages, all the way through high school. This strategy demonstrates the best that research has to offer for stopping inappropriate behavior.

Strategy ▶

Other Noncoercive Strategies

The following are examples of other noncoercive response strategies that can be used to respond to inappropriate student behaviors that are of consequence. Remember, the main objective of all response strategies is to "stop" inappropriate behavior by getting the full attention of the student, then "redirect" student actions to an appropriate activity.

Strategy ▶

Reevaluate the Situation

One of the first steps you should take when a student or group of students is behaving inappropriately is to reevaluate the situation. If you have a group of students that won't quit talking, step back and see if you can determine why they are talking. Perhaps they do not understand the assignment and are trying to figure it out together. Maybe something has happened at lunch that needs to be addressed. If you find that this is the case, you may need to deal with the disruptive event, reteach the objective, or perhaps even restructure the assignment to be completed as a class or in small groups.

Strategy ▶

Reinforce Appropriate Behavior

Recognition and praise reinforce students who are behaving appropriately. Phrases such as, *"Thank you for raising your hand, Andy,"* and *"I appreciate that Jose, Su-Ling, and Monica followed my directions so quickly,"* or tangible rewards such as points and tickets provide motivation and incentives to behave appropriately. Overlooking inconsequential off-task behaviors and giving attention to students who are meeting expectations will create a positive classroom atmosphere where all students have a reason to behave appropriately.

Strategy ▶

Proximity

Proximity is an easy to use strategy for dealing with many inappropriate behaviors. If a student or group of students is off-task or disrupting the class, move closer to the student or group in incremental steps. As you *"move toward the problem,"* often the behavior will change, and students will comply with expectations without you even saying a word.

Restate Expectations

◀ Strategy

Sometimes students are off-task or behave inappropriately because they do not fully understand your expectations or the related consequences. Often restating the expected behavior, motivators, and consequences, followed up by a check for student understanding is all it takes to get a class back on-task.

Example: *"It is important for everyone to behave appropriately as you work on this assignment. Please listen as I restate the expectations for this activity. The expectations are: put your feet on the floor, turn your bodies facing forward, and work silently. If you have a question or need help, please raise your hand and I will come to your desk. Students who meet these expectations will receive a ticket (or other motivator). Leroy, please repeat for the class the behavior that is expected during this activity."*

State the Facts

◀ Strategy

In some situations, stating the facts will motivate students to behave appropriately. For example, if you suspect students have switched seats make a statement to the effect that it is better for everyone involved if you know the students' correct names as listed on the seating chart. Explain that this information would be vital in the case of an emergency and will also help to ensure that the wrong student doesn't get blamed for inappropriate behavior when you write your report to the permanent teacher at the end of the day.

Acknowledge and Restate/I Understand

◀ Strategy

Some students may vocally express negative opinions, inappropriate views, and frustrations. Verbally acknowledging a student's comment, validates them as a person and will often diffuse an emotionally charged situation. Phrases such as, *"I understand,"* or *"I can tell that you,"* and *"It is obvious that,"* can be used to acknowledge what the student said without getting emotionally involved yourself. Transition words such as "however" and "nevertheless" will bring the dialogue back to restating the expected behavior.

Example: *"I can tell that you are not very interested in this topic, nevertheless the assignment is to construct a timeline for the industrial revolution and you are expected to have it completed by the end of class."*

Strategy ▶

Remove, Identify, and Redirect

In some instances, it is best to remove the student from the situation before addressing the behavior. Since it is necessary for you to maintain supervision over all of the students in the class, removal of the student should take them out of earshot, but allow you to maintain visual contact with the rest of the class. Calmly ask the student to go to the front or back of the room, or into the doorway. Direct the class to resume their work, then approach the student. Stay calm and in control of the situation. Identify the rule that was broken or explain that their behavior was unacceptable. State the consequences and go on to explain the consequences if the behavior continues. Express your confidence in the student's ability to behave appropriately, have the student restate what is expected of them, and then return to their desk and begin working.

Strategy ▶

Consequences

Another aspect of responding noncoercively to inappropriate behavior is the implementation of consequences. Many times you will teach in classrooms where the permanent teacher has already established consequences for behavior. Using these established consequences helps maintain continuity of the learning environment for students and makes it so that you don't have to develop consequences of your own. In situations where you do have to devise and implement consequences, keep the following in mind:

I understand

There are two words that can stop most protests from any student and let you take control of the situation. These words are, "I understand."

If a student says, "But that's not fair!" you can say, "I understand, however, that's the way it is."

If a student says, "I hate you!" you can say, "I understand, however, I am the teacher today and you are expected to follow my directions."

If a student says, "This assignment is stupid," you can say, "I understand, nevertheless you will need to have it completed for class tomorrow."

I Understand: Two simple words that no one can argue with.

- When possible, consequences should be a natural outcome or directly related to the behavior. For example, if a student is off-task and doesn't finish their assignment, the consequence could be that they are required to work on the assignment while the rest of the class participates in a fun activity.

- Consequences and their implementation should not provide undue attention to misbehaving students.

- What is a negative consequence to one student may be a reinforcing consequence to another. If the consequence doesn't change the behavior, change the consequence.

- Consequences should be administered quickly and quietly without getting emotionally involved.

- All consequences should be reasonable, appropriate, and in accordance with district or school guidelines and policies.

Consequences should always be made known to students before they are administered. In other words, consequences should not be sprung on students out of nowhere after the behavior has already taken place. Students need to know in advance what they can expect as a result of their behavior, both positive and negative, so they can make informed choices about how to behave. Consequences should be communicated to students as predetermined outcomes of behavior rather than threats. It is a good idea to discuss consequences in conjunction with explaining expectations for the classroom or particular activity.

Effective Discussion of Expectations & Consequences

Teacher: *"During today's science activity, you will be using water and working with syringes at your desk. I expect you to use the syringes, water, and other materials appropriately as outlined in the activity. Anyone who uses these materials inappropriately will be asked to leave their group and observe the remainder of the activity in a seat away from the lab area."*

Teacher: *"Jordan, what is it that I expect during this activity?"*

Jordan: *"To use the syringes, water, and other materials appropriately as outlined in the activity."*

Teacher:	*"Shelley, what are the benefits of using these materials appropriately?"*
Shelley:	*"I can remain with my group and complete the activity."*
Teacher:	*"That is right. What will be the consequences if someone uses the materials inappropriately, Tyrel?"*
Tyrel:	*"They will be asked to leave their group and watch the rest of the activity from a seat away from the lab area."*

Correct Individuals

When necessary, you should correct individuals and implement consequences at the individual student level rather than punishing the whole group. Punishing the entire class for the misbehavior of one student usually results in two negative outcomes. First, the student receives a lot of attention as they are singled out and recognized as the cause for the class consequences. Second, any trust you had established with the remaining students is lost due to your unfair actions. By correcting and applying consequences to an individual, that student receives direction and is not over recognized for their negative behavior.

Challenging Scenarios

The following are four challenging situations you might encounter. Suggestions on how to respond to them in a noncoercive, calm, and proactive manner are included.

Responding Noncoercively to a Refusal to do Work

In some classrooms, you may have a student or students who refuse to complete assignments or participate in activities. Your first response should be recognition of students who are on-task and positive encouragement for the noncompliant student. If after you encourage the student to complete the assignment, they make a statement such as, *"You can't make me,"* an appropriate strategy would be to acknowledge and restate. Disarm the student by acknowledging that he or she is correct, then restate your expectations and consequences if they are not met.

Example: *"You're right, I can't make you complete this assignment. I can, however, expect you to have it completed before recess. If it is not finished by then, you will stay in and work on it. I also expect you to remain quiet and not disrupt the other students who are choosing to complete the assignment at this time."*

It is important to note that many times a refusal to do work is an indication that students don't know how to complete the assignment. They would rather appear bad, than stupid. If this is the case, you may need to reteach the concept or provide extra assistance to the student. Emphasize what the student can do or has already accomplished and recognize student effort.

Responding Noncoercively to Inappropriate Language/ Derogatory Remarks

At times, students may use profanity or make a derogatory remark about you, another student, or the permanent teacher. In such situations, it is important that you try not to take the remarks personally, respond to the behavior in a professional manner, and don't let your emotions override your behavior management skills.

The classroom expectations and consequences established at the beginning of the day have provisions for dealing with this challenging situation — Implement them! You might say something like, *"Susan, you chose to break the classroom rule regarding using appropriate language. What is the consequence?"* The student should then state the consequence and it should be carried out. Do not ask the student why they said what they said (you really don't want to know), just acknowledge that the student *chose* to break a rule or behave inappropriately and implement an appropriate consequence. Dismiss the incident as quickly as possible and resume class work.

Responding Noncoercively to a Fight

Should you see two students yelling at each other, or poised for a fist fight, respond quickly and decisively, do not hesitate to get help from another teacher if needed.

Verbal jousting can usually be extinguished by a firm command as you move toward the problem saying, *"I need both of you to take a quiet seat,"* or *"Stop this right now and take a quiet seat against the wall."* Your calm, authoritative voice combined with an instructive statement will most often yield compliance to your directive.

If students are engaged physically, you must quickly, and with authority, tell them to step back away from each other. Placing yourself between the students may stop the engagement, but can be dangerous for you. Do not get angry, excited, or show a lot of emotion, this will compound the situation. When given firm and instructive directions, students will usually respond and comply as requested.

Responding Noncoercively to Threats

Threats are difficult to handle, the best strategy and response will vary with each situation. However, should a student threaten you or another student, the most important thing you must do is to stay calm and emotionally detached so you can evaluate and manage the situation professionally.

Threat Strategy 1: Acknowledge and Redirect

A threat is often the result of an emotional response. Ignoring the student will probably evoke more threats, and perhaps even aggression. Responding with threats of your own may accelerate the confrontation. The sooner the threat is acknowledged and the situation diffused, the better. Once the student has calmed down you can then direct their actions to something constructive. If you feel the student needs to discuss the situation, it is often wise to wait until after class, later in the day, or refer the student to a school counselor so that emotional distance and perspective on the situation can be achieved.

Example: *"I understand that you are very angry right now. However, I need you to sit down and begin completing page 112 in your math book. We will discuss this situation after lunch."*

Threat Strategy 2: Get Help!

If you feel that you or any of the students are in danger of physical harm, stay calm and immediately send a student or call the office to elicit the help of a permanent teacher or principal. After help has arrived and the situation is under control, document the occurrence. Record what happened prior to the threat, what you said and did, what the student said and did, as well as the involvement or actions of anyone else in the situation.

Skill #5: The ability to avoid being trapped.

There are seven traps in which educators, including substitute teachers, often get themselves caught. Once "trapped" teachers lose some of their power to be a effective educators. Recognizing and avoiding these traps will help provide students with a better learning environment, and avoid a lot of classroom management stress.

Trap #1: The Criticism Trap

Students require attention. Whether they get attention for being "good" or "bad" they will get attention. The criticism trap refers to a situation where the more students are criticized for their inappropriate behavior, the more likely they are to behave inappropriately, in order to continue getting attention from the teacher.

▶ **Criticism / Negative Interactions**

"That's not what I told you to do."

"You've done the whole assignment wrong."

"I've never taught in a class this noisy before."

"I don't want to say this again. Go to work!"

"Didn't you read the instructions?"

Traps to Avoid
- The Criticism Trap
- The Common Sense Trap
- The Questioning Trap
- The Sarcasm Trap
- The Despair and Pleading Trap
- The Threat Trap
- The Physical and Verbal Force Trap

How to Avoid the Criticism Trap

By recognizing and providing reinforcement for appropriate behavior, the need for students to act out in order to get attention is virtually eliminated. As a general rule, teachers should never have more than one negative or critical interaction with a student for every four or five positive interactions.

▶ **Positive Interactions**

"Thank you for following directions."

"You have the first five problems right."

"I'm glad you remembered to put your name on the top of the page."

"I can tell you were listening because of your correct answers."

"You have accomplished a lot this morning."

Trap #2: The Common Sense Trap

The common sense trap is also known as the reasoning or logic trap. It is a situation where common sense, reasoning, and logic are used to try and persuade a student to change their behavior. The reason this strategy is ineffective is that the student doesn't learn anything they don't already know, nor are they offered a single reasonable incentive to change the behavior.

▶ **Getting Caught in the Common Sense Trap**

"Nicki, let's go over this again. As I explained earlier, you should have your assignment completed by the end of class. Look at how much you've got left to do. You keep telling me that you'll get done in time, but unless you go to work you never will. It's up to you to get it done. If you don't complete your assignments, you're going to have a lot of homework."

How to Avoid the Common Sense Trap

Avoiding the common sense trap involves creating a positive environment where there are incentives to change and where positive consequences reinforce that change.

▶ **Avoiding the Common Sense Trap**

"Nicki, you have done the first four problems right. However, I can see that you still have a lot of this assignment left to complete. In order to participate in the end of the day activity, you will need to hurry and finish your work. I'll be back in a few minutes to see how you are doing."

Trap #3: The Questioning Trap

For the most part, questioning students about inappropriate behavior is useless and counterproductive. There are three reasons for not questioning a student about their behavior. First, you really don't want an answer, you want to change the behavior. A student can answer your question and still not comply with the way you want him/her to behave. Second, one question usually leads to more pointless questions that accomplish nothing and waste educational time. Third, as you question a student about an inappropriate behavior, you are actually calling attention to and reinforcing the behavior you want to eliminate. This attention may strengthen the behavior and increase the probability that it will occur again.

▶ **Answers to Questions that Don't Change Behaviors**

Teacher: *"Why did you hit Doug?"*

Student: *"I hit him because he is ugly and I was trying to fix his face. You see my long-term goal in life is to be a plastic surgeon and make ugly people beautiful. Since I haven't yet learned the precise surgical skills needed to do this, I am doing the best I can for a boy my age."*

In this (admittedly absurd) illustration, the student answered the question but it didn't accomplish anything. The teacher gained no new information to help in changing the problem behavior and has probably been incited to ask further useless, infuriating questions.

▶ One Pointless Question Leads to Another

Teacher:	*"Why aren't you working on your assignment?"*
Student:	*"Because I don't want to."*
Teacher:	*"Why don't you want to?"*
Student:	*"It's stupid."*
Teacher:	*"What's stupid about it?"*
Etc.	

How to Avoid the Questioning Trap

As tempting as it may be, don't ask students questions about their inappropriate behavior unless you really need the information to redirect the behavior. A better approach is to restate the expected behavior, have the student demonstrate an understanding of the expectation, then positively reinforce the expected behavior as was discussed in Skill #4, *Dealing Noncoercively with Inappropriate Behavior.*

Trap #4: The Sarcasm Trap

Probably nothing lowers a student's respect for a teacher more than does the use of sarcasm. Belittling students with ridicule destroys a positive classroom environment and may prompt them to lash out with inappropriate remarks of their own. The use of sarcasm suggests that you as the teacher do not know any better way of interacting and sets the stage for similar negative interactions between students themselves.

▶ Getting Caught in the Sarcasm Trap

Teacher:	*"My, my aren't you a smart class. It looks like by age 12 you have all finally learned to find your own seats and sit down after the bell, and to think it only*

*took you half of the morning to do it. I
don't know if there is another class in
the entire school as smart or quick as
you guys."*

How to Avoid the Sarcasm Trap

Avoiding the sarcasm trap is easy; do not use sarcasm!
Better ways of communicating with students are discussed
throughout this chapter.

▶ **Communicating Without Sarcasm**

*"One of the expectations of this class is
to be seated and ready to go to work
when the bell rings. I appreciate those
of you who were quietly seated when
the bell rang today."*

Trap #5: The Despair and Pleading Trap

The despair and pleading trap involves making desperate
pleas to students and asking them to "have a heart" and behave
appropriately. Teachers often become their own worst enemies
when they communicate to students that they feel inadequate
and incapable of managing the classroom and need help.

There will be days when nothing you do seems to work. As
tempting as it may be to confide your feelings of inadequacy and
frustration to the students and plead for their help in solving
the problem, it will rarely accomplish the desired outcome.
More often than not students will interpret your pleas as an
indication that you have no idea what you are doing and the
inappropriate behavior will accelerate rather than diminish.

▶ **What the Despair and Pleading Trap Sounds Like**

Teacher: (With a distraught expression and
hopeless voice) *"Come on, can't you
guys do me a favor and just be quiet for
the rest of class? I've tried everything I
know to get you to behave and nothing
has worked. What do you think I
should do? How can I get you to be
quiet?"*

Student: *"Don't ask me, you're the teacher!"*

How to Avoid the Despair and Pleading Trap

The best defense against the despair and pleading trap is a good offense. Come to the classroom prepared with several classroom management strategies. For some classes, positive verbal reinforcement will be enough to gain compliance. In others, you may need to introduce tangible reinforcers such as point systems, end of the day drawings, or special awards (see page 96 for ideas). When you find that one strategy isn't working with an individual or class, don't be afraid to try something else.

▶ **An Option to the Despair and Pleading Trap**

Teacher: *"Between now and the end of class, I am going to be awarding points to groups who follow my instructions and are on-task. At the end of class, the group with the most points will get to choose a reward."*

Trap #6: The Threat Trap

Threats are just one step beyond despair and pleading on the scale of helplessness. The majority of threats are either inappropriate or unenforceable. They are typically hollow expressions of frustration which tell students that the teacher is at wit's end, out of control, and in over his or her head. Unreasonable and out-of-control threats may sound intimidating, but if students choose to call your bluff you will lose control of the situation because you can't carry out the consequence you've established. You should never threaten consequences that are unenforceable or unreasonable.

▶ **Getting Caught in the Threat Trap**

Teacher: *"If you don't sit down and be quiet right this minute, I'm going to call your parents and have them come and sit by you for the rest of class!"*

How to Avoid the Threat Trap

The best way to avoid frustrating situations that may evoke threats is to formulate and state both expectations and appropriate consequences in advance. Then reinforce appropriate student behavior and administer established consequences as needed.

> ▶ **Avoiding the Threat Trap**

Teacher: *"During this group activity, you are expected to remain in your seat and work quietly with other group members. Should you choose not to do this, you will not be allowed to participate with your group in the review game at the end of the activity."* Wait several minutes for students to comply. *"Group number three is doing an excellent job of staying in their seats and working quietly."*

Trap #7: The Physical and Verbal Force Trap

The use of physical and verbal force, except in instances where life or property is at risk, is absolutely inappropriate; certainly, it is far less appropriate than the behavior that it is intended to stop. Physical force in the classroom as a behavior management tool is not only unproductive, and inappropriate, in many states it is also illegal.

> ▶ **Example of Physical Force**

Teacher: *"I told you to take your seat."* Teacher pushes student into their desk. *"Now stay there until class is over."*

Avoiding the Physical and Verbal Force Trap

Concentrate on restating the expectation in a proactive way then have the student restate and demonstrate the expectation. Keep your cool, count to ten, walk to the other side of the room, do whatever it takes to keep from resorting to force.

The Seven Traps Conclusion

The use of any trap-related management strategies is evidence of an unprofessional, frantic, desperate, even drastic

attempt at managing student behavior. While trap-related strategies may result in initial student compliance, over time they are certain to backfire and result in the steady deterioration of the school and classroom environment.

Behavior Management Summary

By gaining an understanding of basic human behavior and utilizing the skills discussed in this chapter, you will be better prepared to more effectively manage the behavior of students in the classroom. Reviewing this chapter often will assist you as you continue to develop and expand your repertoire of classroom and behavior management skills.

Five Skills for Effective Behavior Management

1. The ability to teach expectations.

2. The ability to get and keep students on-task.

3. The ability to maintain a high rate of positive teacher-to-pupil interactions and risk-free student response opportunities.

4. The ability to respond noncoercively to inappropriate behavior that is consequential.

5. The ability to avoid being trapped.

   - The Criticism Trap

   - The Common Sense Trap

   - The Questioning Trap

   - The Sarcasm Trap

   - The Despair and Pleading Trap

   - The Threat Trap

   - The Physical and Verbal Force Trap

Classroom and Behavior Management involves using techniques and implementing strategies that foster appropriate student behavior in the classroom.

Other Stuff You Should Know

Chapter 3

Introduction

This Chapter is a compilation of important topics which as a substitute teacher you should know about, including:

- Safe Schools
- First Aid & Safety
- Legal Aspects of the Job
- Disabilities and Special Education
- Gifted and Talented Students
- Multiculturism
- Alternative Learning
- Evacuation and Other Out-of-Classroom Activities

The information presented here is only an overview of general guidelines. As you review this information, you may think of additional questions relating to these or other topics. Don't be afraid to ask fellow teachers, school administrators, or district personnel about anything you would like to know. You should take the initiative to learn about specific district policies and state laws.

For additional tips on preparing yourself and becoming a Professional Substitute Teacher, visit:

http://subed.usu.edu

Safe Schools

Most school districts have established a **Safe Schools Policy** to foster a safe environment for students, staff, community, neighbors, and visitors where learning can take place without unnecessary disruptions.

Although each district will have its own version/edition of a Safe Schools Policy, some general guidelines usually apply.

School administrators should have a school-wide behavior management program in place at the beginning of the year, including:

Administrators, staff, teachers, and substitute teachers all have the responsibility and liability of ensuring that the Safe Schools Policy is enforced.

A variety of positive reinforcements

A variety of consequences for inappropriate behavior

A plan for serious misbehavior

High visibility of teachers, staff, and administration

Early intervention programs

Special training programs

Parent involvement

Written policies on expulsion and suspension

Accommodations for special needs students

Help make your school a safe place to work, learn, and play!

Students have requirements and restrictions that foster safe schools, including:

Knowing and complying with the school's rules of conduct

Complying with all federal, state, and local laws

Showing respect for other people

Obeying people in authority at the school

Your district's Safe Schools Policy may be included with your substitute teaching manual. If not, be sure to request a copy from your district office and review it thoroughly.

First Aid

Most classroom and playground accidents should be handled with common sense. Students who are injured should be sent to the office where a school nurse or secretary can administer first aid. Don't fall into the *"band-aid"* or *"ice"* trap, where students are continually asking to go to the office for ice or band-aids for fake injuries. In the event of a severe injury, **do not** move the student. Remain with the student, send another student or teacher for help, and try to keep the other children calm.

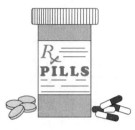

You should never give medication to a student, not even aspirin. If a student requires medication, it should be administered through the school nurse, secretary, or other designated medical personnel.

Learn how to handle situations involving blood and other bodily fluids. Listed below are the OSHA Universal Precautions for dealing with these situations. Contact the school district to find out their specific policies and procedures which should be followed.

OSHA Universal Precautions for Handling Exposure to Blood/Bodily Fluids

1. *All blood/bodily fluids should be considered infectious regardless of the perceived status of the individual.*

2. *Avoid contact with blood/bodily fluids if possible. Immediately notify the school nurse, administrator, or his/her designated first aid person.*

3. *Allow the individual to clean the injury if possible.*

4. *If it is not possible for the individual to clean the injury, disposable gloves should be worn. Gloves are to be discarded in a designated lined bag or container.*

5. *Clothing that has been exposed should be placed in a plastic bag and sent home with the individual.*

6. *Upon removal of gloves, hands should be washed thoroughly with warm water and soap.*

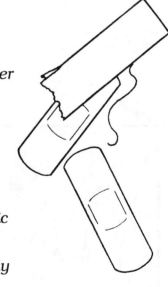

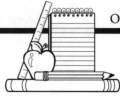

7. *Surfaces contaminated with blood/bodily fluids should be cleaned thoroughly with disinfectant. The cleaning should be completed by the custodian, administrator, or his/her designated individual responsible for clean-up.*

As a general rule: **Do not touch a student who is bleeding even if you use gloves.** For example, if a student has a bloody nose or cut knee, hand them the box of tissues or paper towel, and instruct them to hold it on their wound, then send them to the office or infirmary for further care. Students who are bleeding should not be allowed to participate in class activities until the bleeding has stopped and the wound has been cleaned and completely covered.

First Aid

- Handle accidents with common sense.
- Only the school nurse or other designated personnel should administer first aid including dispensing medication.
- Do not move a severely injured student.
- Learn school district policy for handling situations involving blood/bodily fluids.
- Always remain with the class and send a student or another teacher to get help when needed.

Advice from School Nurses for Substitute Teachers

Berks County Intermediate Unit
Reading, PA

1. Do not dispense medication (prescription or over-the-counter) to any students. Send them to the office or school clinic where they will have a record of the written permission to give the student the medication, the prescribed amount, and a system for recording the times and dosage administered.

2. Refer all students with injuries (even minor ones) to the office so the normal school procedures can be followed. In an emergency, you may need to escort the student to the office. Or, in a less serious situation, have another student accompany the injured child.

3. Carry to school each day a pair of disposable gloves that are waterproof and made of either latex or vinyl, in the event of an emergency that requires you to come in direct contact with a student's injury.

4. Always wear protective gloves when you come in contact with blood, bodily fluids, and torn skin, or when handling materials soiled with the same.

5. If you come in contact with bodily fluids from a student, throw your gloves away in a lined garbage can. Better yet, first seal the soiled gloves in a small plastic bag before depositing them in the trash. Wash your hands for 10 seconds with soap and warm water after you remove the gloves.

6. Encourage students to wash their hands before meals and when using the restrooms to reduce exposure to germs.

7. Do not allow students who are bleeding to participate in class until the bleeding has stopped and the wound has been cleaned and completely covered.

8. Check with the school office when there is a student injury. Some schools may require that you complete an accident report form. If so, leave a copy for the permanent teacher, and keep one for your records.

9. Prevention is the most important antidote for medical emergencies. Always stay with the students. Contact another adult if you need to leave the students at any time. If you have recess duty, walk around the playground being proactive about potentially dangerous behavior. Remember, you are the adult in charge.

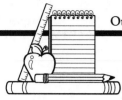

Legal Aspects of the Job

An overall consideration when substitute teaching is your legal responsibility in the classroom and school. The following are some legal responsibilities you should be aware of. An understanding of these responsibilities will require some questioning on your part as to specific school/district policies.

- **Supervision Of Students** — The substitute teacher who has physical control of a classroom has a duty to keep these children safe and orderly. In many states, a teacher acts *in loco parentis* — in the place of a parent — and is allowed to use his/her judgment in a manner similar to a parent. The standard is the reasonable use of professional judgment for the safety and orderly education of students.

- **Due Care And Caution** — A teacher is required to exercise due care and caution for the safety of the students in his/her charge. Essentially, this means acting reasonably and with safety in mind, being able to explain circumstances and your actions, as well as following school safety policies and procedures.

- **Release Of Children** — Due to possible restraints on who may have custody of a child, children should not be allowed to leave the building during the school day without express consent from the office.

- **Administering Medication** — Medication should only be administered by the school nurse or other appropriate health personnel, not the classroom or substitute teacher. If you know of medication requirements of a student, the health professional should be notified.

- **Confidentiality** — It is unprofessional and against the law in many states to disclose confidential information about your students. Generally, a substitute teacher should avoid comments about individual students that convey private information: grades, medical conditions, learning or discipline problems, etc.

- **Anecdotal Records** — Maintaining notes on particular incidents in the classroom can protect you in problematic situations. If you feel that your actions might be questioned, note the date and time, the individuals involved, the choices for action considered, and the actions taken.

- **Discipline Policies** — A substitute teacher should know the state's position on corporal punishment and the school's policy over various aspects of discipline. Some states require a school to have a policy, and often these policies indicate a specific person such as the principal as disciplinarian. If in doubt, referring students to the building principal is sound advice. When sending a student to the principal due to discipline matters, the substitute teacher maintains the duties of supervision and due care for both the individual child and the remainder of the class. Proper action may be detailed in school policy or may require your independent sound judgment. Possible actions include having another child accompany the child, sending a child to bring someone from the office to intervene, or having another teacher watch your class while you take the child to the office.

- **Dangerous Situations** — A substitute teacher is responsible for making sure the learning environment is safe. This includes things such as the arrangement of desks so as not to block exits and proper supervision during the use of potentially dangerous classroom equipment. A teacher must also consider the potential for problems in certain kinds of classes. Planned activities in a physical education, science, shop, or home economics class may be uncomfortable for the substitute teacher. In such cases, the substitute teacher may choose to do an alternative activity which they feel they can conduct safely.

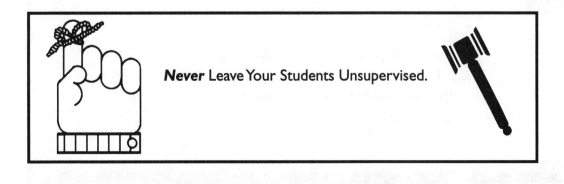

Never Leave Your Students Unsupervised.

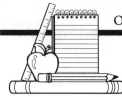

Child Abuse Reporting

Purpose

The purpose of child abuse reporting legislation is to protect the **best interests of children**, offer protective services to prevent harm to children, stabilize the home environment, preserve family life whenever possible, and encourage cooperation among the states in dealing with the problem of child abuse.

Any person, official, or institution required to report a case of suspected child abuse, sexual abuse, or neglect and fails to do so is guilty of a class B misdemeanor.

Duty to Notify

Any school employee (including a substitute teacher) who knows or reasonably believes that a child has been neglected, or physically or sexually abused, should **immediately notify** the building principal, the nearest peace officer, law enforcement agency, or office of the State Division of Human Services.

It is not the responsibility of school employees to prove that the child has been abused or neglected, or determine if the child is in need of protection. Investigations are the responsibility of the Division of Human Services. Investigations by education personnel prior to submitting a report should not go beyond that necessary to support a reasonable belief that a reportable problem exists.

IT'S THE LAW!

Persons making reports or participating in an investigation of alleged child abuse or neglect in good faith are immune from any civil or criminal liability that might otherwise arise from those actions.

Everything you always wanted to know about sexual harassment*

What is sexual harassment?

Definition: Unwelcome sexual advances, requests for sexual favors, and other verbal or physical conduct of a sexual nature when:

1. submission to such conduct is made, either <u>explicitly</u> or <u>implicitly</u>, a term or condition of a person's employment or a student's academic success

2. submission to or rejection of such conduct by an individual is used as the basis for employment or academic decisions affecting such individuals

3. such conduct unreasonably interferes with an individual's work or academic performance or creates an intimidating, hostile, or offensive working, or learning, environment

What is a "yardstick" for determining what constitutes sexual harassment?

Sexual harassment is behavior that:

1. is unwanted or unwelcome

2. is sexual in nature or gender-based

3. is severe, pervasive and/or repeated

4. has an adverse impact on the workplace or academic environment

5. often occurs in the context of a relationship where one person has more formal power than the other (supervisor/employee, faculty/student, etc.)

Sexual Harassment is illegal. Don't do it- Don't tolerate it!

To whom can I talk about sexual harassment concerns?

1. Your local principal, superintendent, or personnel/ human resources office

2. Your City or State office of Anti-Discrimination

3. Your State office of Equal Employment Opportunity Commission (EEOC)

4. The Office of Civil Rights, U.S. Department of Education

but were afraid to ask

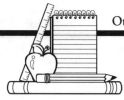

What are some examples of verbal, non-verbal, and physical sexual harassment?

The following are behaviors which <u>could</u> be viewed as sexual harassment <u>when they are unwelcome</u>:

Verbal
- whistling or making cat calls at someone
- making sexual comments about a person's clothing or body
- telling sexual jokes or stories
- referring to an adult woman or man as a hunk, doll, babe, or honey
- spreading rumors about a person's personal sex life
- repeatedly "asking out" a person who is not interested

Non-verbal
- paying unwanted attention to someone (staring, following)
- making facial expressions (winking, throwing kisses, licking)
- making lewd gestures
- giving gifts of a sexual nature

Physical
- hanging around, standing close, or brushing up against a person
- touching a person's clothing, hair, or body
- touching oneself in a sexual manner around another person
- hugging, kissing, patting, stroking, massaging

What should I do if I feel I am being sexually harassed?

Sexual harassment can be directed at, or perpetrated by you, administrators, faculty members, staff members, or students.

1. Talk to your harasser if possible. Tell her/him that you find the behavior offensive.

2. Continue going to work/classes.

3. Document all sexual harassment incidents. Record the time, date, place, and people involved.

4. Consider talking to others to see if they have experienced sexual harassment.

5. Put your objection in writing, sending a copy by registered mail to the harasser and keeping a copy in your file. Say:

    a. On "this date" you did "this."

    b. It made me feel "this."

    c. I want "this" to happen next (i.e., I want "this" to stop).

6. Report the harassment to the building administrator and district personnel/human resource director.

Disabilities and Special Education

Inclusion: Placing children with mild, moderate, or severe disabilities in regular education classrooms.

Five affective, or attitudinal benefits:

1. The nondisabled learn to be more responsive to others

2. New and valued relationships develop

3. Nondisabled students learn something about their own lives and situations

4. Children learn about values and principles

5. Children gain an appreciation of diversity in general

If the child is able to participate in school activities, academic lessons, lunchroom activities, recess, games, etc., he/she MUST be included.

Public Law 94-142

Passed in 1975, **"The Education for All Handicapped Children Act"** has been amended and is now called **"IDEA"** or the "Individuals with Disabilities Education Act." It provides that all handicapped children between the ages of 3 and 21 are entitled to **free public education**. Presently, the terms **disability** and **disabled** are used <u>in place of</u> handicap and handicapped.

Nearly 20% of All children 3-17 have one or more developmental, learning, or behavioral disorders. This means 1 in 5 have a social or learning problem that requires special attention!

The law defines disabled individuals to include those who are *mentally retarded, hard of hearing, deaf, speech-impaired, visually handicapped, seriously emotionally disturbed, or orthopedically impaired; have multiple handicaps; or have other health impairments or learning disabilities* and therefore need special educational services.

IDEA also provides that ALL students with disabilities have the right to be served in the **least restrictive environment** - this means that disabled children must be educated and treated in a manner similar to their nondisabled peers. This usually consists of **mainstreaming** which is placing disabled children in the regular classroom.

Who decides which children are disabled and, if so, how they will be educated? Federal Law requires that a team consisting of the student, his/her parent(s), teachers, principal, and other professionals develop an **IEP** (individual education plan)

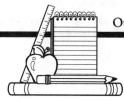

detailing the goals and objectives of the educational services to be provided. The IEP lists all special and regular activities that the student will participate in.

Federal Law states that NO ONE has access to a student's IEP without the parent's permission. It is always a good idea to check with the permanent teacher and/or administrator, preferably before taking over a classroom, to determine how best to deliver educational services.

Students with disabilities in one area may be capable or even exceptional in others. By eliminating or modifying barriers to participation, students with disabilities may enjoy regular classroom activities and assignments.

Adapting games and activities for students with disabilities

Guidelines

1. Often, children with disabilities already know their capabilities and limits – simply encourage them and be ready to assist if needed

2. Focus on children's abilities - not disabilities

3. It is okay to modify the game/rules to meet the needs of the <u>entire</u> group

4. Keep the game/activity as complete and original as possible

5. Be sensitive, especially with new students/disabilities - start slowly and develop gradually

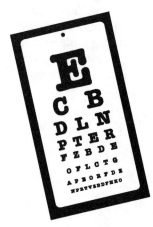

Ideas for adapting games/activities

-   Reduce the size of the playing area

-   Adjust the boundaries, change the number of players, lower the net

-   Use walls, fences, or designated "helpers" to aid in keeping the ball in-bounds

-   Find bigger/lighter equipment

-   Incorporate plastic bats, rubber racquets, jumbo gloves, enlarged hoops, expanded goals, etc.

- Substitute beach balls, nerf balls, whiffle balls, bladder balls, styrofoam balls, balloons, etc.

- Slow it down

- Throw underhand, roll the ball, bounce the ball, hold the ball still, use a batting tee, etc.

- Allow an "extra" bounce, count before throwing, use "left" (or right) hand, no hands, etc.

Adapting assignments and activities for student with disabilities

Under the Americans with Disabilities Act, Passed in 1992, you could be sued for a civil rights violation if you withhold services or programs from a child with disabilities.

Guidelines

1. Generally, the permanent teacher and/or resource person will already have policies in place. Find out what they are and use them

2. Focus on the children's abilities – not disabilities

3. It is okay to modify the assignment for certain students and not others

4. Keep assignments as similar to the rest of the class as possible

5. Be sensitive, especially with new students/disabilities – start slowly, develop gradually

Ideas for adapting activities/assignments

- Reduce the number of pages or questions

- Half the page or problem, every other page or problem, the first page or problem, the last page or problem, only pages or problems with pictures, pick your own pages or problems

- Reduce the difficulty of activities/assignments (barriers due to physical or emotional disabilities)

- Read out loud, write on board, use overheads, move desk for better hearing, seeing, and monitoring, speak more slowly, speak louder, repeat, rephrase, redirect instructions and questions

- Increase confidence, compassion, and cooperation

- Use lots of examples, use "warm-ups," model, review, practice, practice, practice; I do one & you do one; I do part & you do part, provide patterns or steps to follow

- Be patient and smile

Advice from Special Educators for Substitute Teachers

Berks County Intermediate Unit
Reading, PA

In some cases, you may be assigned to teach in a special education "resource room" where all of the students have been identified as having special needs. In other cases, you may be teaching in a regular classroom where there are particular students with identified special needs. Whichever is the case, here are some thoughts on how to facilitate the learning of these students.

1. Respect is the key attitude for success with all students.

2. These students may have a variety of learning challenges. Do not think first of their special needs, but think of them first as learners.

3. All children respond to sincere encouragement, but don't overdo it. Be sensitive to the fact that learning is more difficult for these students than for many others.

4. Depending on the grade level you are teaching, these students may have experienced years of school failure. Be aware of this as you respond to their needs and work to help them find success.

5. Depending on the student's learning challenge, you may find you need to repeat yourself more often. Be patient. Check for student understanding after giving directions.

6. If there are problems, do not single out a child in front of the class, but deal with him/her privately.

7. Many children with special needs have Individualized Education Plans (IEPs). Consult these plans when available, as they provide structure for the students' learning. The teacher should have daily plans drawn from these IEPs.

8. You often may be privy to confidential information about students with special needs. It is critical that all information you obtain about students during your teaching day remain confidential. Depending on the grade level, students may feel self-conscious that you know they have learning challenges, this can set up a defensiveness on their part.

9. During your teaching day, you may need to locate yourself in close proximity to these children to offer assistance and help them stay focused. A gentle reminder will oftentimes suffice for them.

10. An instructional assistant or aide may be in the classroom. Such a person can be of tremendous help because they have a history with the students and are aware of routines, personalities, and other important background information.

11. Do not hesitate to ask for assistance from the principal or another teacher if you have concerns or questions during the day.

12. Carefully note the daily schedules for special needs students. They often have support personnel (language or hearing specialists) come into the classroom. At other times, they may leave the classroom to attend regular or special classes.

13. There may be specialized teaching equipment or machines in special education classrooms. Check with the instructional assistant, the principal, or another teacher before using these items.

14. Sometimes students are allowed to use certain learning aids to assist them with their work. Hopefully, the regular teacher will leave information instructing you as to which students may use the aids, and under what circumstances.

15. In some special education classes, behavior reports go home daily to parents that record the behavior of the child throughout the day. Become as familiar as possible with the system, or ask the assistant to focus on or give the feedback for the particular student(s) for the day.

16. In class discussions, if a student responds with an incorrect answer, provide clues or a follow-up question to help him/her think of the correct answer. Look for ways to praise students for their thinking and behavior as well as correct answers.

17. Present short and varied instructional tasks planned with students' success in mind.

18. Have on hand an ability-appropriate book to read, audio tapes, flash cards of facts, games, puzzles, mental math exercises, or other activities for substituting in these classes.

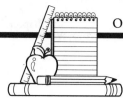

Gifted and Talented Students

Gifted and talented students usually have above average ability, a high level of task commitment, and highly developed creativity. Many children will excel in one of these areas. Truly gifted children will excel in all three.

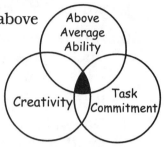

(Renzulli model)

You may have a gifted student if she or he...

_____ has a vocabulary noticeably above her or his peers

_____ is a voracious reader – usually more advanced content

_____ has a well-developed sense of humor – gets jokes peers don't understand

_____ is intrinsically motivated – works hard with or without teacher approval

_____ has a personal standard of quality – independent of others' work

_____ thinks at a higher/independent level – often appears to "day dream"

_____ is able to go beyond basic lesson concepts – expand, elaborate, and synthesize

Often gifted and talented students seem to be round pegs in square holes. They do not necessarily fit the mold of an "ideal student." They may become bored with class or deeply involved with something unrelated to the lesson. Their friendships and alliances include a need for intellectual peers (often older students or adults) and chronological peers (kids their same age). Moreover, their attention span does not always coincide with the standard time allotments for classroom lessons and activities.

Some Do's and Don'ts When Working with Gifted and Talented Students

Do

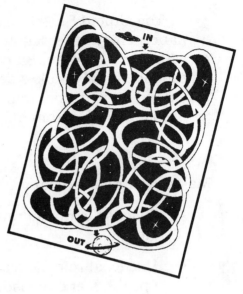

✓ Enrichment and extension activities

✓ Puzzles and games

✓ Alternative projects (collages & posters are good)

✓ Comparisons, similes, and analogies

Don't

✗ make them do things they've already mastered

✗ give them busy-work if/when they finish early

✗ force them to always work with slower students

✗ have them memorize, recite, and copy

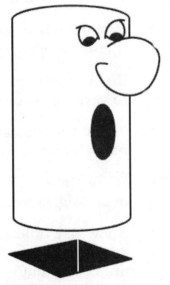

Multiculturalism

The United States is home to a diverse population. No other nation enjoys the rich and varied cultural heritages found within our borders. Since this diversity is reflected in our schools, it only makes sense that our instructional methods should benefit from and be sensitive to the special abilities and needs of people from different groups.

Making your classroom multicultural friendly

General definitions of Terms

Ethnic Diversity:
Similarities and differences of groups of people classified according to common traits, values, and heritage. Examples may include food, clothing, music, and rituals.

Racial Diversity:
Similarities and differences of groups of individuals with certain physical or genetic features. These features may include skin color, body type, and facial features.

Cultural Diversity:
Similarities and differences of groups and/or individuals that align themselves with others based on common racial and/or ethnic characteristics or affiliations. Typical associations often include language, customs, and beliefs.

- Discuss various groups' heritage, values, and practices/rituals

- Use local role models from various groups as guest speakers and advisors

- Plan activities that use materials/objects that reflect various customs and cultures

- Honor each student's unique background/heritage and how it enhances society's characteristics

- Encourage discussion of current topics and how they relate to various groups within our society

- Present stories and/or artifacts from different groups as a basis for various activities

- Write stories, sing songs, draw pictures, or play games depicting various cultural influences

- Showcase different groups' contributions and/or participation involving historical events, literary works, art, music, medicine, sports, and industry

Showing respect for your students' heritage and beliefs -as well as your own- will encourage your class to be more accepting of you and others and will create a positive and cooperative learning environment.

Alternative Learning

We are all different. We look differently and we act differently. We also learn differently. Unfortunately, we tend to teach students as if they were all the same. We all know of people that can't bounce a ball, but can do math story problems in their heads – or the person with two left feet that can sing like a bird. No one can do everything, but most of us do excel in one or more areas. It is in these areas that we learn best. By using a variety of teaching methods and activities that incorporate these abilities, we can increase students' ability to stay on-task, pay attention, and enjoy learning.

Here are some main categories of skills and abilities with just a few examples of each:

Verbal/Linguistic
Reading/writing
Vocabulary
Speech

Logical/Mathematical
Calculation
Formulas
Codes

Visual/Spatial
Imagination
Patterns/designs
Sculpture/painting

Body/Kinesthetic
Dance
Drama
Sports/games

Interpersonal
Group work
Empathy
Cooperation

Intrapersonal
Self-reflection
Thinking strategies
Reasoning skills

Musical
Rhythms
Sounds/tones
Singing/playing

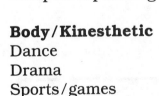

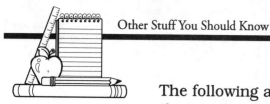

The following are ideas for new ways to teach "old" materials that might appeal to your students' particular abilities and interests:

Math

- compose a song to help remember a formula

- "illustrate" the problem on the board

- solve the problem as a group

Language

- Act out the story

- Write key words using a code

- Listen with eyes closed

History

- Reenact a battle

- Write a commercial for that time period

- Do a mock interview of an historical person

Gym / P.E.

- Research and play an historic game

- Keep score using Roman numerals or fractions

- Skip or hop instead of running

Running out of ideas?

Ask your students how they can turn a writing assignment into a math assignment, or how they can incorporate art into a soccer game. You'll be surprised at the results and your students will enjoy the challenge.

Evacuation and Other
Out-of-Classroom Activities

In addition to regular classroom management, there are several special situations which you need to be aware of and prepared for. These situations include emergency and evacuation procedures; assemblies; playground and lunch duty; field trips; inclement weather days; and escorting students to the bus. As you review the following suggestions, keep in mind that you are the teacher, and as such assume full responsibility for all of the students in your care.

Emergency and Evacuation Procedures

- Ask the district office for information about emergency action plans and protocol. Find out what to do in the event of fire, flood, earthquake, bomb threat, etc.

- Since every building and classroom is different, it is important to know where the nearest exit is, and have a class list available to grab when you evacuate the building.

- If you hear the fire alarm or a message over the intercom, instruct the students to quickly and quietly leave the room in single file, heading for the designated exit door.

- Some classrooms now have an "emergency backpack" hanging by the door. If you see such a backpack, take it with you when you evacuate.

- After evacuating the building, use the class list to account for all of the students in your class.

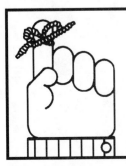

Most Important: Evacuate the students in your classroom and have a class list with you as you leave the building.

Assemblies

At first thought, an assembly seems like a pleasant break in the school-day routine. However, it can turn into a nightmare for a substitute teacher who does not have a plan for managing students during this activity. Here are some suggestions to help you survive the event with nerves still intact.

1. Find out the time and location of the assembly, and whether or not the students will need to bring chairs from the classroom. In a middle school, you should also check to see how the regular class schedule will be altered to accommodate the assembly.

2. Talk to neighboring permanent teachers. Many schools have specific procedures for going to and returning from an assembly, as well as assigned seating for each class.

3. If such procedures exist, familiarize yourself with them and do your best to follow them.

4. If there are no established procedures, devise your own (walk in a single file line down the hall to the assembly, sit together as a class, return in a single file line, etc.).

5. Determine the specific behavior you expect during the assembly, with consequences and rewards dependent upon how these expectations are met. Beware of punishing the whole class for the misdeeds of a few. This can create a hostile environment with the students acting out against each other as well as you.

6. Teach or review with the students the procedures, expected behavior, and consequences or rewards associated with the activity.

Field Trips

- A field trip is a method of providing students with first-hand learning opportunities. Field trips are often used to introduce or conclude a specific topic of study. As a substitute teacher called on the day of a field trip, you have many duties in order to successfully carry out the planned learning experience.

- Parental permission to participate in the field trip must be secured prior to the trip. Be certain that such permission, usually a signed release/consent form, has been obtained for all of the students in the class.

- Find out the school policy for any students who do not have documented parental permission to participate in the field trip. If a student without permission is required to remain at school, it is often arranged for them to attend another teacher's class.

- Student behavior is an important part of any educational experience. Prior to the trip reiterate with the students some do's and don'ts of expected behavior.

Do
* be courteous
* stay with the group
* listen attentively
* follow safety regulations

Don't
* ask personal or irrelevant questions
* lag behind
* interrupt
* take samples or touch, unless given specific permission to do so

- Since you will most likely be unfamiliar with the students, create name tags to be worn on students' shirts or coats. If you are visiting a location where there may be many school groups, use a distinctive shape or color for your students' name tags.

- Students should be assigned a travel partner, and chaperons should be given a specific group of students with a list of their names. You may want to consider giving each chaperon's group a different color name tag.

- Safety precautions must be considered at all times. Take a first aid kit along.

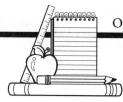

- Count the number of students before leaving the classroom and often throughout the excursion, especially when loading and unloading buses or moving from one area to another.

- Students should have been informed of special things to look for and what they will likely see and hear on the trip. Familiarize yourself with the learning agenda, if possible, and use this information to facilitate student learning on the trip.

- Means of note-taking may have been planned for upper grade students. This may include using clip boards, taking notebooks, or completing specific note-taking sheets prepared for the trip. Do your best to carry out the plans left by the permanent teacher.

- Follow the planned time frame and sequence for the visit. Set aside time for note-taking, questions and answers, or sketching as needed.

- Processing the trip is essential for true learning to take place. On the return trip or back at school, have students share what particular experiences interested them. You may also want to follow up with a summative writing assignment.

- Remember, you are responsible for the supervision and conduct of your students at all times, including on the bus and at the field-trip destination.

Playground & Lunch Duty

Being on playground or lunch duty involves more than just physically being in the vicinity of the students. Your job is to supervise their actions and activities to ensure a safe environment and experience. Take proactive measures to deter potential problem situations. Intervene before situations get out of control. Should a serious problem arise, don't hesitate to elicit help from another teacher or school administrator, send a student to get this help. Never leave a group of students unsupervised.

Inclement Weather Days

In the event of inclement weather, schools often have different procedures for students during lunch and recess. Often teachers are expected to return to the classroom with students after lunch or keep them in the classroom during recess. Be sure to find out what is required of you so that your students are adequately supervised. Have several activity ideas in your **Super SubPack** to keep students constructively occupied in the classroom.

Escorting Students to the Bus

In some schools, you may be expected to escort students from the classroom to the bus. Find out exactly what is expected. Do you walk the entire class out and at what time? Do you need to stay in the bus loading area until the buses have left? What about students who don't ride a bus? Every school is different, and sometimes even classes within the same school have different bus policies. Do your best to find out what you need to do from the office, neighboring teachers, or students before the end of the day.

Teaching Strategies, Skills, and Suggestions

Chapter 4

Introduction

Have you ever had difficulty teaching the lessons left by the permanent teacher, tried to line up a class of 30 active second graders, or realized that you are spending a small fortune on good behavior rewards and thought to yourself, "there must be a better way?" There is! Chapter Four, *Teaching Strategies, Skills, & Suggestions,* is filled with tips and suggestions from the files of permanent and substitute teachers. It includes:

- Suggestions for the contents of your **Super SubPack**

- Strategies for presenting the permanent teacher's lesson plans

    - Brainstorming

    - Concept Mapping

    - KWL

    - Cooperative Learning

    - Questioning

    - Effective Implementation of Audio Visual Materials

- Ideas for low cost/no cost rewards and motivators and many other helpful hints from experienced teachers who have been there, done that, and have some great advice to offer.

For additional information regarding Teaching Strategies, visit:

http:// subed.usu.edu

Suggested Contents For Your
Super SubPack

Classroom Supplies

- ❐ Crayons
- ❐ Rubber bands
- ❐ Markers and/or colored pencils
- ❐ Labeled ball-point pens (red, blue, black)
- ❐ Pencils and small pencil sharpener
- ❐ Transparent and masking tape
- ❐ Scissors
- ❐ Glue sticks
- ❐ Paper clips, staples, a small stapler
- ❐ Post-it Notes® (various sizes and colors)
- ❐ Ruler
- ❐ File folders
- ❐ Calculator
- ❐ Lined and blank paper
- ❐ Name tag materials (address labels or masking tape will work)

Personal/Professional

- ❐ Clipboard
- ❐ Substitute Teacher Report
- ❐ District information (maps, addresses, phone numbers, policies, starting times, etc.)
- ❐ Coffee mug or water bottle
- ❐ Whistle (useful for P.E. and playground duty)
- ❐ Small package of tissues
- ❐ Snack (granola bar, pretzels, etc.)
- ❐ Individualized Hall Pass
- ❐ Small bag or coin purse for keys, driver's license, money (enough for lunch), and other essential items. Do not bring a purse or planner with a lot of money, checks, and credit cards (there may not be a secure place to keep it).
- ❐ Band-aids
- ❐ Small sewing kit with safety pins
- ❐ Disposable gloves and small plastic bags

Rewards/Motivators

- ❐ Candy
- ❐ Mystery Box
- ❐ Tickets
- ❐ Certificates
- ❐ Stickers
- ❐ Stamp and Ink Pad
- ❐ Privilege Cards (get a drink, first in line, etc.)

Activity Materials

- ❐ The *Substitute Teacher Handbook*
- ❐ Tangrams
- ❐ Bookmarks
- ❐ "Prop" (puppet, stuffed animal, etc.)
- ❐ Picture and activity books
- ❐ A number cube or dice for games
- ❐ Estimation jar
- ❐ Newspaper
- ❐ Timer or stopwatch

Super SubPack

A **Super SubPack** is like an emergency preparedness kit for the classroom. It should contain a variety of useful and necessary classroom supplies and materials. The contents of a **Super SubPack** can be organized into four categories: Personal and Professional Items, Classroom Supplies, Rewards and Motivators, and Activity Materials. The specific contents of your **SubPack** will be personalized to fit your teaching style and the grade levels you most often teach.

SubPack Container

When selecting a container for your **Super SubPack**, choose one that is easy to carry, large enough to hold all of your supplies, has a secure lid or closure device, and looks professional.

Super SubPack Contents

Most of the suggested **Super SubPack** contents listed on page 70 are self-explanatory. The following is a brief explanation of some of the not-so-obvious items:

Bookmarks: Bookmarks are a fun lesson extension that can be used with any reading activity (see page 191).

Clipboard: Carrying a clipboard will provide quick access to a seating chart, the roll, and anecdotal records, as well as convey a sense of authority.

Disposable Gloves & Plastic Bags: Whenever you encounter blood or bodily fluid you should wear disposable gloves to help safeguard against many of today's medical concerns. A plastic bag can be used in an emergency when you must dispose of items exposed to blood or bodily fluids.

Estimation Jar: Estimation jars are great

motivators for students to behave appropriately and complete assignments efficiently so they can earn guessing tickets (see page 97).

Mystery Box: Place a common item such as a toothbrush or piece of chalk in a small box. Allow students to lift, shake, smell, and otherwise observe the box throughout the day. At the end of the day, have students guess what is in the box and award a small prize to the student who identifies the contents correctly (see page 120).

Newspaper: A newspaper can be used as the basis for a story starter, spelling review, current events discussion, and a host of

other activities (see page 198).

Props: A puppet, magic trick, or even a set of juggling props can capture student interest. Props provide great motivation to complete assignments in order to participate in, learn more about, or see additional prop-related activities.

Tangrams: Tangrams are geometric shapes that can be used as filler activities, as well as, instructional material to teach shapes and geometry (see page 144).

Tickets: Tickets are a great way to reward students for appropriate behavior. Students can use tickets to enter an end of the day drawing or redeem them for special privileges and prizes.

Brainstorming

Brainstorming is an essential part of teaching creativity and problem-solving processes that form the basis for active learning. With younger children, it makes sense to compare a brainstorm to a rainstorm.

Can you feel and count the individual drops of rain in a rainstorm when the rain begins to fall? (Yes)

As the storm gets bigger and bigger, can you count the drops of rain? (No)

A brainstorm is like that too, only we are going to use our creative minds to think of many, varied, and unusual ideas; so many that we will hardly be able to write them down quickly enough.

There are four simple rules that help make the brainstorming process a peaceful and orderly one. Teach these **"DOVE"** rules to the students:

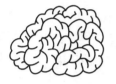

D Don't judge others' ideas – evaluation comes later.
O Original and offbeat ideas are encouraged.
V Volume of ideas – as many as possible in time limit.
E Everyone participates.

It is very common for students to run out of ideas in a short amount of time. This is called "hitting the wall." Help students keep thinking, because the most interesting, and unusual ideas, often come after the immediate and obvious ones have been expressed. You may have a student read their list in order to help others start thinking of new ideas. Remind students that it is okay to "piggyback" on someone else's ideas. Often a really unique idea from one person can spark another good idea from someone else.

It is important in brainstorming to limit the time. A shorter time limit is better than one that is too long. One to three minutes is usually about right, occasionally up to five minutes might be needed. It is better to start with a short time and extend the activity than to have the students lose interest.

Brainstorming can be very useful when teaching students about creativity. Brainstorming new and crazy uses for an object teaches students to be flexible in their thinking. The following examples work well:

- Brainstorm uses for a pencil.
- Brainstorm uses for a set of keys.
- Brainstorm all of the things that would be in the perfect classroom.

Brainstorming at the beginning of a lesson is a good way to introduce the lesson and assess what students know about the topic, as well as being a method of channeling their thinking in a specific direction.

Depending on the topic of the lesson, brainstorm attributes or facts that relate to the lesson.

- Brainstorm things that are red (or read).
  . . . things in your home that are man-made, things that are natural.
  . . . things in the classroom that are geometric shapes.
  . . . things that live in the ocean, names of birds or flowers, insects, folktales, etc.

Brainstorming is also very effective as one of the steps in problem-solving and solution-finding situations:

- What problems might you have if you came home from school and were locked out of the house?
- What might happen if an earthquake destroyed your city?
- What are a variety of ways that you can prepare for a test?
- What are some things you can say to friends who want you to smoke, drink alcohol, or take drugs?

Brainstorming can also be used to help children evaluate an idea. For example, brainstorm all of the possible consequences:

- What if a light bulb that lasted 20 years was invented?
- What if the sun didn't shine for a year?
- What if students were required to wear school uniforms?
- What if school buses were allowed to have advertising on them?
- What if you ran for school president and won?
- What if your mother let you eat all of the junk food you wanted?

After many ideas have been generated, use those ideas to advance the objectives of the lesson. For example, if you brainstormed the consequences of eating all of the junk food you wanted, a lesson on nutrition might follow.

Evaluation of brainstormed ideas should not happen during the brainstorming process. If someone says *"Boy, that won't work"* or *"That's a stupid idea,"* then ideas are squelched and some students will stop participating. If evaluation is a step you want to use, it comes later after all ideas have been freely given.

Concept Mapping

Like brainstorming, concept mapping can be used to introduce a topic. It can also be used to evaluate what students have learned at the conclusion of a lesson.

As an introductory exercise, concept mapping provides you with information regarding what the students already know. You won't waste time covering the material they are already familiar with and can concentrate your efforts on presenting new information.

As a follow-up activity, concept mapping illustrates the learning that has taken place. It is fascinating to compare pre-lesson concept maps with post-lesson concept maps. Both you and the students will be amazed at how much they have learned.

Example of a Concept Map:

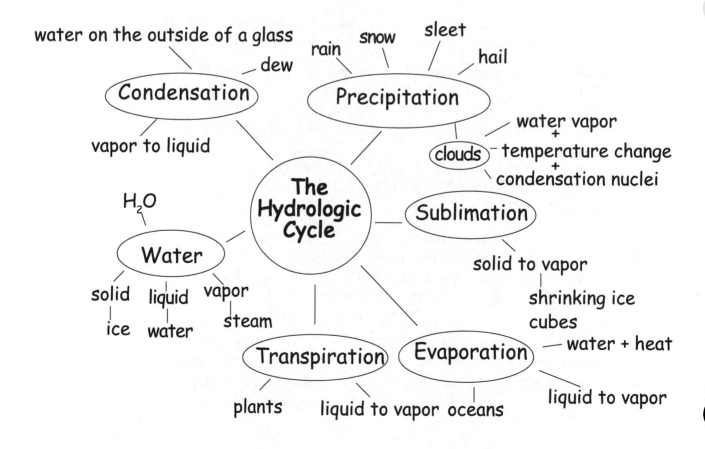

Concept mapping usually involves placing a word or idea in the middle of the board or on a piece of paper. Students then share what they know or associate with this concept. The information volunteered by the students is recorded with lines drawn to show how different concepts are related to one another. Concept maps can either be developed by the entire class, in small groups, or on an individual basis.

Concept mapping is also an effective method of reviewing information. It requires students to synthesize information they have read, heard, or observed and restate it in a concise manner using key words and terms which they understand. Once students have identified what they know in a concept map, another effective exercise is to have them incorporate examples and applications of the information into their map.

Both brainstorming and concept mapping can be used with any topic at any grade level. In either exercise, it is imperative that you as a teacher cultivate a risk-free classroom environment where students are not afraid to share their thoughts and ideas.

K-W-L

A major challenge of substitute teaching, particularly in the upper grades, is trying to teach a subject you know absolutely nothing about. One method of providing a meaningful learning experience in such a situation is the utilization of a KWL Chart. KWL stands for "what do I **K**now," "what do I **W**ant to know," and "what have I **L**earned." A KWL chart provides an outline for having students teach you. As you are being taught, the students will be teaching each other, and clarifying concepts in their own minds.

A lesson using KWL would begin by the teacher listing the letters K, W, and L across the top of the board. Under the appropriate letter would be written, "what do I know," "what do I want to know," and "what have I learned" (see page 77). The teacher then lists facts which they know about the subject in the first column. In the second column, the teacher lists things they want to know or understand. A brief look at a student textbook will help to list "want to know" topics and ideas which students will be capable of addressing. Students are then asked to help answer and explain the items listed in the "W" column. Encouraging students to refer to their textbooks and other resources to answer your questions will help ensure that correct principles are being taught and explained.

At the end of the class period or lesson, the teacher completes the final column, listing what they have learned during the class from the students, with students checking to make sure the "learned" information is correct.

South America

An example K-W-L Chart that could be used for learning about volcanoes:

K What do I **Know**?	W What do I **Want** to know?	L What have I **Learned**?
1. Lava comes out of volcanoes. 2. There are volcanoes in Hawaii. 3. Volcanoes erupt. 4. The lava from volcanoes is hot. 5. Volcanoes can be dangerous.	1. What is lava? 2. Where does lava come from? 3. Where are most of the volcanoes in the world? 4. Why do volcanoes erupt? 5. etc.	1. Lava is melted rock. 2. When lava is still under ground, it is called magma. 3. etc.

An adaptation of this teaching method is to have students complete individual KWL charts (see page 78). This works well with assignments such as reading science chapters or watching videos. Before the activity, students write down what they know and what they want to/think they will learn during the activity. At the end of the activity, they complete the third column. A class discussion of the information students list in the third column will help clarify any confusing points and provide a review of the material covered.

K-W-L

K
What do I **Know**?

1.
2.
3.
4.
5.
6.
7.
8.
9.
10.

W
What do I **Want** to Know?

1.
2.
3.
4.
5.
6.
7.
8.
9.
10.

L
What have I **Learned**?

1.
2.
3.
4.
5.
6.
7.
8.
9.
10.

Cooperative Learning

Many teaching strategies and activities call for students to work together in small groups. This is often referred to as "cooperative learning." In cooperative learning, the teacher acts as a facilitator rather than a presenter. Students learn as they interact with and teach each other.

Outlined below are instructions for a simplified version of cooperative learning developed by Dr. Carolyn Andrews-Beck called "Bargain Basement Group Work."

1. Group students. Have students count off or form groups based on the seating arrangement. Do not let student self-select groups. Keep the groups small, usually between two and five students per group.

2. State the objective and instructions for the group work, then have students do the following:

   a) Circle - Arrange themselves in a small compact group so that they can all see everyone else's face.

   b) Introductions - Have students state their name to be sure everyone in the group knows each other.

   c) State the assigned task - The job is . . . .

   We will know we are done when . . . .

3. Set a time limit for the activity.

4. Have students begin working together towards accomplishing the objective outlined in step number two.

Assigning roles to students is also helpful in facilitating learning. By giving each member of the group a specific assignment, you guarantee their involvement. Students who are actively involved are more likely to learn.

Common Role Assignments:

Director, Captain, Leader, or Manager: The group leader responsible for keeping the group members on-task and working towards the objective.

Recorder: Records information for the group's activities, fills out worksheets, or prepares written material from information provided by the group.

Materials Manager: Responsible for obtaining and returning equipment, materials, and supplies necessary for the activity.

Procedure Director: Reads instructions, explains procedures, makes sure the activity is being carried out correctly.

Clean-up Leader: Supervises the clean-up of the group's area at the end of the activity or project.

Setting Up a Cooperative Learning Activity in the Classroom

Group Students	Teacher: Starting with Cherice and going up and down the rows please count off by fives.
	Cherice: One
	Next Student: Two
	Next Student: Three, Etc.
	Teacher: I would like all of the "ones" to bring a pencil and paper and form a circle by the door. I would like all of the "twos" to bring a pencil and paper and form a circle by the bulletin board in the back of the room. I would like all of the "threes". . . . Please move to your assigned location and form a circle now.
State the Objective and Instructions for the Group	Teacher: In your groups you are going to make up a two minute skit about one of the reasons we have listed on the board why kids shouldn't start smoking. After you have made up the skit and had a chance to practice it, each group will present their skit for the rest of the class. Who can tell me what the assignment is? Noah?
	Noah: Use one of the reasons for not smoking on the board to make up a skit for the class.
	Teacher: How will you know when your group is done? Trish?
	Trish: After we have practiced our skit and are ready to present it to the class.
Set a Time Limit	Teacher: You will have 15 minutes to make up and practice your skit before we begin the class presentations.
Establish Roles & Have Students Begin Working	Teacher: Identify the person in your group who is wearing the most blue. This person will be the skit director, they are responsible for selecting a reason from the board and making sure everyone has a part in the skit. The person sitting to the right of the director will be the time monitor who makes sure your skit isn't more than 2 minutes long and that your group is ready to present in 15 minutes. Everyone else will help develop the skit and be actors. Are there any questions? . . . . O.K., you may begin.

Questioning

Good questions lead to good thinking - and good thinking leads to learning.

Good questions should:

- Be developed logically and sequentially

- Be adapted to students' abilities

- Cause students to think - not merely recite

- Encourage students to ask questions

Good questions will:

- Help keep students on-task and focused

- Help determine skill and knowledge levels

- Promote higher level thinking

- Encourage broader student participation

A Basic Rule . . . Ask, Pause, Call
Too often, good questions fail to be valuable because:

A) Teachers don't allow enough time for the questions to be answered. Teachers frequently ask a question and then go ahead and answer it themselves - students quickly learn that they do not have to think or respond.

B) Teachers fail to direct their questions to specific students. They give a question to the entire class which often makes it scary or "uncool" for any one student to volunteer to answer.

Using the (Ask, Pause, Call) method will increase the effectiveness of your questions.

ASK   A well thought out question to the class

PAUSE   Long enough for students to think about a response

CALL   On a specific student to respond to the question

Pauses Cause Them to Think

The 1ˢᵗ pause gives the entire class time to formulate an answer

The 2ⁿᵈ pause provides the student time to verbalize a response

The 3ʳᵈ pause encourages the student and/or class to really "get into" the question

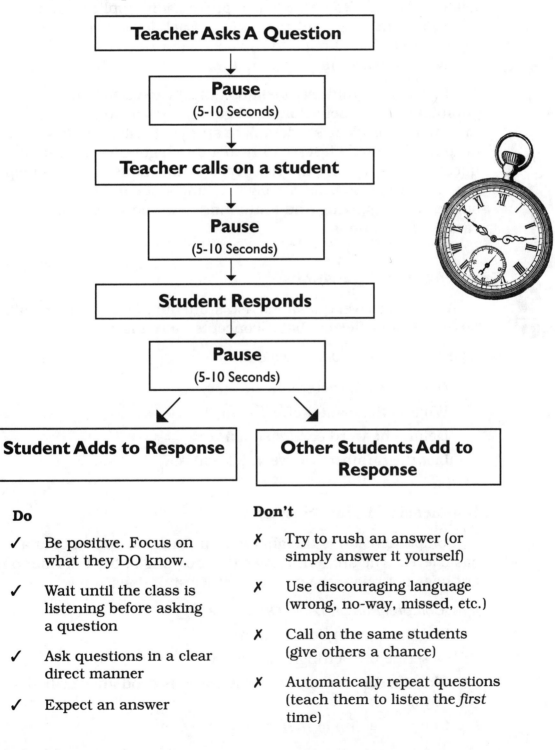

Teacher Asks A Question

↓

Pause (5-10 Seconds)

↓

Teacher calls on a student

↓

Pause (5-10 Seconds)

↓

Student Responds

↓

Pause (5-10 Seconds)

↙ ↘

Student Adds to Response	**Other Students Add to Response**

Do

✓ Be positive. Focus on what they DO know.

✓ Wait until the class is listening before asking a question

✓ Ask questions in a clear direct manner

✓ Expect an answer

Don't

✗ Try to rush an answer (or simply answer it yourself)

✗ Use discouraging language (wrong, no-way, missed, etc.)

✗ Call on the same students (give others a chance)

✗ Automatically repeat questions (teach them to listen the *first* time)

Questions to Promote Higher Level Thinking

Effective questions keep students thinking and involved in the learning process. Dr. Benjamin Bloom divided thinking into six levels commonly known as Bloom's Taxonomy. The levels range from simple knowledge to complex evaluation in the following order: knowledge, comprehension, application, analysis, synthesis, and evaluation. Each level involves a higher level of thinking and thus a greater degree of student involvement with the subject matter.

Higher level thinking questions can be used to help stimulate class discussions and give greater meaning to information or ideas students are studying. All students, despite their grade level, can respond to higher level thinking questions. By asking the right type of questions, you can help students progress from merely recalling facts and figures, to successfully applying and evaluating new information in a variety of situations.

Knowledge Level Questions

Knowledge level questions ask students to recognize, recall, and state facts, terms, basic concepts, and answers.

Sample Knowledge Level Questions

> Name the characters in the story.
>
> What is the capitol of Wyoming?
>
> Define the word *condensation*.
>
> List the numbers between 23 and 45.

Comprehension Level Questions

Comprehension is the ability to understand concepts at a basic level. The student knows the meaning of the information, but does not relate or apply it to other situations.

Sample Comprehension Level Questions

> List three examples of plants.
>
> Describe the setting of the story.
>
> Classify the characters in the story as good guys or bad guys.
>
> Compare a cup of milk with a cup of water.

Application Level Questions

Application is the ability to use learned knowledge in particular and concrete situations. The student can apply rules, principles, and concepts in new and appropriate contexts.

Sample Application Level Questions

Why is the sun important to life on Earth?

Using what you have learned, how would you solve the following problem?

How would schools be different if there was no electricity?

How much money would you have if you saved a dollar a day for seven years?

Analysis Level Questions

Analysis is the ability to breakdown a concept into its component parts.

Sample Analysis Level Questions

Why did the boy in the story give away his gold coin?

Diagram the parts of a flower.

Explain the differences between a raindrop and a snowflake?

Which characters in the movie were necessary for the plot?

Synthesis Level Questions

Synthesis is the ability to put together elements or parts so as to form a whole. The student arranges and combines pieces to form a pattern, structure, or idea that was not clearly evident before.

Sample Synthesis Level Questions

How could you change the characters' personalities to make them more likable?

Design a new invention for . . .

Organize the books you have read this year into three categories.

Prepare a shopping list for Thanksgiving dinner.

Evaluation Level Questions

Evaluation is the ability to judge the value of materials, methods, or ideas. This level of thinking requires the highest level of intellectual functioning. It requires students to not only understand the material but to also make a judgment based on this understanding.

Sample Evaluation Level Questions

Should students be allowed to bring cell phones to school?

Would you recommend this book/movie to a friend? Why?

How would the discovery of life on another planet affect the U.S. Space Program?

Does the protection of endangered species justify the loss of job opportunities?

Verbs Often Used to Promote Higher Level Thinking

Level of Thinking	Typical Verbs Used	Examples of Teacher Questions
Knowledge	define draw repeat record identify label list name	*Name* the author of the book.
Comprehension	classify compare contrast translate explain summarize give examples	*Compare* the weather today with the weather yesterday.
Application	apply calculate complete demonstrate illustrate practice solve use predict show	*Complete* the sentence using a vocabulary word from the lesson.
Analysis	analyze classify discuss divide explain infer inspect	*Explain* why it is important to have classroom rules.
Synthesis	arrange combine construct create design develop generalize organize plan predict categorize rearrange	*Predict* what would happen if a law was passed which made commercials on TV illegal.
Evaluation	assess critique estimate evaluate judge rank rate recommend test value justify	What requirements for hiring a new teacher would you *recommend* to the principal?

Effective Implementation of Audio Visual Materials

Many times the lesson plans left by a permanent teacher will include the presentation of audio visual materials such as videos or filmstrips. While audio visual presentations do not thoroughly captivate students as they once did, they can still be an effective means of presenting content material. The key to encouraging learning during the presentation is to involve students as active, rather than passive, viewers. Listed below are five strategies for involving students and conducting effective audio visual presentations.

Keep the Lights On

A darkened classroom is an invitation for problems. As it dulls your mental alertness, it will embolden students to try and get away with things they would never attempt in broad daylight. A well lit classroom is consistent with the traditional learning environment and makes it possible for students to take notes or complete assignments concurrent with the presentation.

Stand in the Back

Another critical aspect of audio visual presentations is what you as the teacher are doing. The students' job is to watch the presentation, your job is to monitor student behavior and learning during the presentation. Sitting behind the teacher's desk correcting papers or reading a book is not an effective means of doing this. Consider standing at the back of the room. Because you are already on your feet, you can easily move to problem areas in the classroom and with proximity stop problems before they start. By positioning yourself behind the students, they cannot see if you are paying attention directly to them; therefore, they must assume that you are and behave accordingly.

K-W-L

Use individual KWL charts such as the one found on page 78. Before the presentation, have students complete the first two columns indicating what they already know about the topic and what they think they will learn. As the video or filmstrip is presented, students write down information they are learning in the third column. After the presentation, have students share what they listed in the third column to create a comprehensive class list of the information that was presented.

Concept Mapping

Assign students to take notes during the presentation in the form of concept maps. Start by listing the topic of the video or filmstrip in the center of the page. As the presentation progresses, they should jot down key words and bits of information they are learning (see the sample concept map on page 74). At the end of the presentation, have students turn in their concept maps for teacher review or give a short quiz on the information during which students are allowed to refer to the concept maps they have constructed.

Question Exchange

Either during or after the presentation, have students write three questions which meet the following two criteria:

1)   the answer to the question must have been given during the presentation,

2)   the student writing the question must know the answer.

At the conclusion of the presentation, students exchange questions and try to answer them.

How Should I Do That?

When substituting, you are expected to cover the material outlined in the permanent teacher's lesson plan. However, sometimes lesson plan instructions are general and very nonspecific with regard to lesson presentation. Here are several techniques for presenting lesson plans that will cover the material in a positive and creative way.

Lesson Plan: *Have students read Chapter 18 and answer questions.*

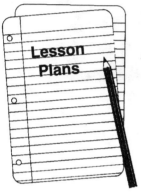

(1)   Pre-test and post-test. Ask students to guess what will be covered before they start reading. Share ideas aloud and write down five facts or ideas as predictions. Afterward, conduct a post-test by checking the accuracy of their predictions.

(2)   Togetherness. Read the assignment out loud with students to find the answers. By making the assignment a class activity, you promote classroom cooperation.

(3)   Group effort. Divide the class into groups and ask each group to report on part of the reading. This method is best used with material that does not require continuity to be meaningful.

(4)   Quiz Board. Give the assignment and tell the students that you will stop 15 minutes before the end of the class and establish a quiz board. Appoint three to five students or select volunteers to be members of the board. Ask them to come to the front of the room. The rest of the students pose questions to these students about the day's reading. After a certain number of questions have been answered, a new board may be selected. This technique works well for review. An added advantage is that you need not know the subject well in order to handle it.

Lesson Plan: *Have the class write a composition about X Y Z.*

(1)   To make any topic more meaningful, encourage students to relate to it personally. One way is to write sentence starters that use the students' natural speech pattern, such as, "I wish," "I like," "I'm glad I'm allowed to," "I think."

(2)   If the students are assigned to write a story, suggest that

they first decide on a cast of characters, a setting, a time, etc., as a class. By doing the groundwork together, the students will be "into" the story before they lift a pencil.

(3)   If the assignment is an essay, consider using a brainstorming technique. Ask students to say whatever comes to mind about the topic and write their ideas on the board in some quick, abbreviated form. When everyone has had a chance to study the list, students can begin to write using whatever brainstorming ideas they wish.

(4)   Whatever the topic, propose that the students write free association word lists about it. Tell them to start with the given word, such as "freedom," "pets," or "winter," and then add up to ten other words that immediately come to mind about the key word. Now the students can write their own compositions.

(5)   Before students start to write, initiate a values clarification exercise that will help students relate an abstract subject to their own lives. For example, if the topic is "conservation of electricity," have the students start by listing five electrical gadgets or appliances they use, that they could do without. Record their answers on the board. From this specific exercise, the students can move on to the broader issue.

Lesson Plan: *The class has a test tomorrow. Have them study and review.*

(1)   Try a game format for drill material, such as spelling, number facts, state capitols, and vocabulary. Use familiar games like tic-tac-toe, Jeopardy, Baseball, etc.

(2)   Have pairs or small groups of students make up model tests. Assign one group true and false questions, another multiple choice questions, etc. Spend the last part of the class going over the questions. Ask each group to read their test, while the rest of the class gives the answers.

(3)   Have the students teach each other:

A.   Give five minutes in which students are to write five to ten things they know about the material covered without opening their books or using their notes.

B.   Ask students to compare their list with the student next to them. In pairs, have them add additional items during the next ten minutes.

C.   Have the students remain in pairs and open their books and notes. Add to their lists using their notes and text during the next ten minutes.

D.   Allow each student pair to join an adjacent pair and ask the groups of four to compare their lists and add additional information during the next ten minutes. Encourage students to discuss and clarify their knowledge.

E.   In a full class discussion, have students consider all known knowledge. Allow students to ask questions of one another and have knowledgeable students clarify misunderstandings.

Lesson Plan: *Discuss topics A B C with class.*

(1) Have a student lead the discussion, or call on two or three students.

(2) Have the class spill out all sorts of ideas related to the discussion topic. Do not judge the ideas - anything goes! Just encourage the students to speak their minds. After about five minutes, start the discussion again, this time arranging their ideas in a more orderly fashion.

(3) If the topic is controversial, divide the class into sections, each representing a special-interest group. During the discussion, each group will give its point of view on the subject.

Lesson Plan: *Show the film or filmstrip, then discuss.*

(1) To heighten student interest in the audio visual materials, use the pre-test and post-test technique. Introduce the activity with a comment such as, "If you were making a movie about crocodiles, earthquakes, or China, what would you include?" As they watch, have students check their lists against the film. How does the film compare to the students' expectations?

(2) As students watch, have them write down three questions that are answered in the film or video, then discuss the questions with the class after the presentation.

For additional audio visual suggestions, see page 88.

101 Ways to Say "Good Job!"

Everyone knows a little praise goes a long way in the classroom. Whether it is spoken or written at the top of a student's paper, praise reinforces good behavior and encourages quality work. But the same traditional phrases used over and over can sound rehearsed and become ineffective. Here are 101 variations of ways to give praise, show interest, and offer encouragement:

1. You've got it made.
2. Super!
3. That's right!
4. That's good!
5. You are very good at that.
6. Good work!
7. Exactly right!
8. You've just about got it.
9. You are doing a good job!
10. That's it!
11. Now you've figured it out.
12. Great!
13. I knew you could do it.
14. Congratulations!
15. Not bad.
16. Keep working on it; you're improving.
17. Now you have it.
18. You are learning fast.
19. Good for you!
20. Couldn't have done it better myself.
21. Beautiful!
22. One more time and you'll have it.
23. That's the right way to do it.
24. You did it that time!
25. You're getting better and better.
26. You're on the right track now.
27. Nice going.
28. You haven't missed a thing.
29. Wow!
30. That's the way.
31. Keep up the good work.
32. Terrific!
33. Nothing can stop you now.
34. That's the way to do it.
35. Sensational!
36. You've got your brain in gear today.
37. That's better.
38. Excellent!
39. That was first class work.
40. That's the best ever.
41. You've just about mastered that.
42. Perfect!
43. That's better than ever.
44. Much better!
45. Wonderful!
46. You must have been practicing.
47. You did that very well.
48. Fine!
49. Nice going.
50. Outstanding!
51. Fantastic!
52. Tremendous!
53. Now that's what I call a fine job.
54. That's great.
55. You're really improving.
56. Superb!
57. Good remembering!
58. You've got that down pat.
59. You certainly did well today.
60. Keep it up!
61. Congratulations, you got it right!
62. You did a lot of work today.
63. That's it!
64. Marvelous!
65. I like that.
66. Cool!
67. Way to go.
68. You've got the hang of it!
69. You're doing fine.
70. Good thinking.
71. You are learning a lot.
72. Good going.
73. I've never seen anyone do it better.
74. That's a real work of art.
75. Keep on trying!
76. Good for you!
77. Good job!
78. You remembered!
79. That's really nice.
80. Thanks!
81. What neat work.
82. That's "A" work.
83. That's clever.
84. Very interesting.
85. You make it look easy.
86. Excellent effort.
87. Awesome!
88. That's a good point.
89. Superior work.
90. Nice going.
91. I knew you could do it.
92. That looks like it is going to be a great paper.
93. That's coming along nicely.
94. That's an interesting way of looking at it.
95. Out of sight.
96. It looks like you've put a lot of work into this.
97. Right on!
98. Congratulations, you only missed . . .
99. Super - Duper!
100. It's a classic.
101. I'm impressed!

The Line Up!

57 ways to get kids in a row

LINE UP IF YOU CAN TELL ME ...

1. what you would wish if you had one wish ...
2. something people don't like: being late, sour milk, flies, noise ...
3. something people do like: rainbows, picnics, hugs, good movies ...
4. a safety rule for home or school: don't play with matches ...
5. a health rule for home or school: cover coughs and sneezes ...
6. the name of a television character or show title ...
7. the name of a state: Missouri, Kansas, Colorado, New Mexico ...
8. where your father works, or mother's occupation ...
9. the name of a city: New York, Boston, Detroit, Chicago ...
10. the name of a country: Scotland, Canada, India, Italy ...
11. what you would like to be when you grow up: an engineer, a news reporter, a pilot ...
12. your favorite subject in school ...
13. your favorite place to visit: the woods, the ocean, the park, the gym ...
14. a book title, author, character, illustrator ...
15. a kind of fruit: banana, plum, grapes ...
16. a kind of vegetable: lettuce, beans, corn ...
17. a type of tree: oak, maple, weeping willow, elm, lilac ...
18. a type of flower: rose, tulip, daisy, iris, marigold ...
19. the name of a movie star, singer, rock group ...
20. your favorite cereal: Cocoa Puffs, Rice Krispies, Raisin Bran, Sugar Smacks ...
21. a hobby or collection: gardening, stamps, stickers, dolls, biking, shells ...
22. an animal in the zoo: an ostrich, panda, monkey, rattlesnake...
23. an animal on a farm: rooster, goat, pig, cow, hen, duck ...
24. where your family went on vacation ...
25. the name of a school worker: Mr. Manors (the cook), Ms. May (the principal) ...
26. your address, phone number, birthday ...
27. what you would do with a million dollars ...
28. one thing you learned in school this week ...

LINE UP IF YOU HAVE ...

29. a tooth missing, two teeth, three, four ...
30. blue as your favorite color, purple, orange ...
31. a T-shirt on, short sleeves, long sleeves ...
32. a ribbon in your hair, a watch on your left arm ...
33. a "Z" in your name, a "B," an "F," a "Q" ...
34. a birthday in January, February, March ...
35. been to a circus, a rodeo, the zoo ...
36. sneakers on, boots, sandals ...
37. two people in your family, three, four ...
38. a pet dog, cat, bird, fish, turtle, horse ...
39. seen the movie *Star Wars, Mulan, Toy Story* ...
40. striped socks on, pink socks, brown socks ...
41. taken dance lessons, Judo, swimming, voice, piano, guitar, flute lessons ...
42. visited California, Florida, Texas, Utah, Arizona ...
43. participated in a wedding as a bride's-maid, flower girl, ring bearer ...
44. flown in an airplane, a helicopter, an air balloon, sailed, motorcycled ...
45. gone snow skiing, water skiing, snorkeling ...
46. cooked hot-dogs, hamburgers, grilled cheese sandwiches, cookies, cakes ...
47. helped parents mow the lawn, wash the car, clean the kitchen ...
48. performed in a recital, play, sports activity for an audience ...
49. moved to a new neighborhood, town, city, state, country ...
50. brought back your library books today, yesterday, tomorrow ...
51. walked to school, rode the bus, the subway, drove with a parent or friend ...
52. been polite to a friend, teacher, parent today ...
53. blue eyes, brown eyes, hazel, black ...
54. been to a hospital for tonsils, broken bones, to visit a friend ...
55. written a poem, story, song, play ...
56. stood on your head, played tag, skipped rope, raced ...
57. a short vowel in your name, a long vowel ...

Low Cost / No Cost
Rewards and Motivators

In the ideal classroom, all students would be intrinsically motivated to behave appropriately and work hard on every assignment. However, this is not usually the case. Many substitute teachers experience success in motivating classes by providing rewards throughout the day. The following are ideas for low and no-cost rewards and motivators.

- **Certificates** Photocopy blank certificates (see pages 98-100) to be filled out and given to exceptional students, groups, or the entire class at the end of the day or as prizes for classroom activities.

- **Pencils and Paper Clips** Colorful variations of these school supply basics are well received at any grade level as contest prizes. They can often be purchased very inexpensively at discount and dollar stores.

- **Stickers** These can be given intermittently throughout the day to students who are on task or placed on completed assignments to denote outstanding work.

- **Tickets** Throughout the day, students can be given tickets for being on-task, cooperating, and following directions. These good behavior tickets are then turned in for a drawing to win a special prize prior to going home (see page 101).

- **Candy** Always a favorite, but be cautious when using it. Some students may have health conditions which do not allow them to enjoy this reward. In addition, many state health codes require that candy be commercially manufactured and individually wrapped. If you do give out candy in the classroom, be sure that the wrappers are disposed of properly.

- **Extra Recess Time** Being allowed five extra minutes of recess can provide tremendous motivation for many students. Be sure to check with the principal or neighboring teacher before hand to make sure that this reward will not interfere with the schedule of anyone else in the school.

- **Privilege Cards** Individual students can be rewarded for good work or appropriate behavior with special privileges. You can make privilege cards that entitle students to things such as being first in line, getting a drink, being the teacher's assistant for an activity, choosing the end of the day activity, etc. (see page 100). When the student redeems the privilege, collect the card and put it back in your **Super SubPack** for your next assignment.

- **Fun Activity** The promise of a fun activity later in the day can motivate students for hours. The activity might be a *Five Minute Filler* or **Short Activity** from this book, or any other activity you think they would enjoy. Remember, being "fun" is usually anything that is different from the routine of an ordinary day.

- **Story Time** One successful substitute teacher uses the promise of a story at the end of the day to motivate classes. She brings to school an old pop-up book about a dinosaur. At the beginning of the day, the word "DINOSAUR" is written on the board. A letter is erased each time the students are off-task or behaving inappropriately. At the end of the day if there is any of the word "DINOSAUR" still left on the board, they get to hear the story. Second-hand book stores are a good place to look for inexpensive books that your students will not have seen before.*

- **Estimation Jar** Fill a jar with pennies, marbles, beans, or rubber bands. Recognize students who are on task, setting a good example, or working hard, by giving them a slip of paper to write their name and guess on. The more times they are recognized for good behavior throughout the day the more chances they will have to "guess." At the end of the day, reveal the total number of items in the jar and award a prize to the student whose guess was the closest.

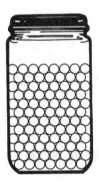

- **Talk Time** Middle school students really like moving to another seat and being allowed to sit and talk with friends during the last five minutes of class. To insure an orderly classroom, you may need to insist that students select their new seat and then not be allowed to get up until class is over. Elementary students also enjoy this activity while waiting to go to lunch or at the end of the day.

Notes For The Teacher:

Establish rewards and motivators not as "bribes to be good" but as "goals" that students can work toward and achieve through good behavior and diligent effort.

Submitted by Marilyn Machosky of Sylvania, Ohio

☆Certificate of Award☆

_____

did an outstanding job _____
today in class!

_____   _____
Date   Teacher

☆Certificate of Award☆

_____

did an outstanding job _____
today in class!

_____   _____
Date   Teacher

☆Certificate of Award☆

_____

did an outstanding job _____
today in class!

_____   _____
Date   Teacher

Congratulations . . .

_____
Name

Was a Winner in the _____ Contest Today!

_____   _____
Date   Teacher

Congratulations . . .

_____
Name

Was a Winner in the _____ Contest Today!

_____   _____
Date   Teacher

Congratulations . . .

_____
Name

Was a Winner in the _____ Contest Today!

_____   _____
Date   Teacher

Super Class
A W A R D

This award is presented to

_____

Class of Super Stars for

_____

Date: _____ **Signed:** _____

Privilege Card

The holder of this card

is entitled to

_____

_____

_____

_____

_____

_____

Authorized Signature

Privilege Card

The holder of this card

is entitled to

_____

_____

_____

_____

_____

_____

Authorized Signature

Getting a . . .

Many substitute teachers are working towards the goal of getting a permanent teaching assignment and classroom of their own. If you are such a substitute, listed below are some suggestions that might help.

- **Be Proactive**

   Meet with principals and district personnel early in the year to let them know that you are excited about working in the district and hope at some point to be offered a permanent teaching position. Let your intentions be known.

- **Be Available**

   Districts are looking for people who they can depend on. Once you have signed up to substitute, try to be available to teach whenever you are needed. Your willingness to fill in at the "last minute" will make a lasting, favorable impression on those who will be making personnel decisions later in the year.

- **Be Professional**

   You are a teacher in the school district. You should act, dress, and speak appropriately. Arrive early and stay late. Volunteer to help with after school activities. If your intentions to become a permanent teacher are known, you will be evaluated for this position in everything you do and say throughout the school year.

- **Avoid Criticism**

   Anything negative you say about a school, principal, or teacher will eventually come back to haunt you. Stay positive and compliment those around you whenever possible. If you can't say anything nice, don't say anything at all.

. . . Permanent Job!

- ## Be Confident

Walk tall, teach with confidence, but don't be overbearing.

- ## Evaluations

When appropriate, ask for positive evaluation forms or letters of support/recognition to be filed at the district office. Many times only negative evaluations are filled out and sent in.

In some districts, up to 25% of the new hires come from the substitute pool.

- ## Learn From Experience

Don't assume that one bad experience or evaluation will take you out of the running. Learn from the experience, ask for advice from other teachers or principals.

- ## Grow Professionally

Attend workshops sponsored by the district. Some districts even invite substitute teachers to attend inservices scheduled for permanent teachers. You may also consider subscribing to current education journals or magazines. This illustrates that you are serious about a career in education and want to stay current with what's happening in the profession. Check with media center personnel for subscription information.

- ## Get To Know The District

One of the most commonly used phrases in prospective teacher interviews is, *"Are you familiar with . . ."* By illustrating your knowledge of special programs, textbooks, or the mission statement of a district, you show that you are interested and up-to-date with what's going on in the district. Applicants who are familiar with district programs and practices have a better chance at getting a job.

For tips on "How to Prepare for the Successful Interview" see Resources under Substitutes, at:

http:// subed.usu.edu

Substitute Hints & Suggestions

1. Know the teacher next door. Introduce yourself so you can call on someone to answer questions about schedules or material for the class throughout the day.

2. When students need to go to the restroom or the library, send only one student at a time. When the first one returns, a second one may go.

3. If there is not a seating chart left by the teacher, quickly make one. It is much easier to maintain discipline when you can call students by name.

4. If a student doesn't respond when you call him/her by name, you may suspect the students have switched seats. Tell them it is better if you have their correct names so the wrong student doesn't get in trouble and written about to the permanent teacher.

5. Do not let students start any name calling or being rude to other students. It is much easier to stop a verbal disagreement than pushing or fighting.

6. Try to be in the hall between classes. It is a good idea to stand in the doorway so you can keep one eye on the hallway traffic and one eye on students coming in the classroom. If the students see a teacher, they are less likely to behave inappropriately.

7. Have a couple of extra pens or pencils with you for students who have "forgotten" and would rather go to their lockers and walk the halls than be in class.

8. If you give a student a pen or pencil and would like it back, be sure to ask the student for his lunch card, or something of value that he/she will be sure to remember they want back. Many students just forget that it isn't their pen.

9. Try to identify the names of one or two trustworthy students who will tell you the truth and help out in class.

10. Never let a class go early for lunch or the next class unless the teacher for whom you are substituting or the teacher next door says it is okay. Some schools have very strict rules about the number of students in the cafeteria/hallways at a time.

11. Never let a student have a pen without an ink cartridge. It possibly will be used as a spit ball thrower.

12. Establish your rules and expectations very clearly at the beginning of the day.

13. Do not let students use a phone in the classroom. Have them use the phone in the office.

14. Do not discuss the teacher's class with other people, especially out of school. You are a professional and shouldn't discuss individual students or problems.

15. If you need to talk to someone about a problem, talk to the principal.

16. Be neat in your appearance.

17. Follow the lesson plans the teacher has left. Incorporate your own ideas if there is extra time.

18. Correct the students' work for the day if possible.

19. Even though a few students can upset your plans, try to find out the names of students who have been good or helpful and let the teacher know about them also.

20. Most students will acquiesce to your leadership, but there will be some who will question your plans or authority. It is better not to argue. Instead say, *"I know this may not be the way Mr. Smith does it, but this is the plan for today."*

21. If you are not sure how the teacher wants an assignment done, ask another teacher or develop your own plan. Then be sure to leave a note for the permanent teacher explaining what you assigned.

22. Be assertive, so students don't feel they can manipulate your decisions and authority. Use statements such as:

> I need you to start reading now.
>
> I want everyone to pass their papers forward.
>
> I don't need...
>
> I don't want...

---

23. Don't let students manipulate you by protesting or saying, *"We never do that!"* Calmly tell them, *"I understand, but today we will read aloud instead of silently."*

24. Walk around the room. Don't just sit by the desk, especially during independent work, or a test. Students will be less likely to talk or cheat when you are close by them.

25. Don't let students wear hats during a test. Sometimes they have been known to write answers in the brim.

26. Don't try to catch a student by grabbing an arm or clothes. They could fall and you could twist his arm, or rip his clothes.

27. Don't let any student have a knife or any other weapon. Have them give it to you and report to the office.

28. Do not touch the blood of a bleeding child. Use a napkin, towel, or a cloth to cover the cut. Have the student put his hand on the cut, until you can get to water or the nurse.

29. If a teacher has classroom sets that are used by the students, be sure to have them all returned before the entire class leaves. It is easier to locate one book or calculator in a class of 30 than trying to find it in the whole school. Hopefully, the calculators or books are numbered and have been assigned in a given order so you know who has the missing book.

30. Don't make statements lightly — "Students remember!"

Thank You For Coming Today!

Fill-In
Activities and
Lessons

Can you come
back
tomorrow?

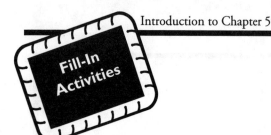

Fill-In
Activities

Fill-In

Activities

and Lessons

Chapter 5

Introduction

As a substitute, it can be difficult to see the big picture and how a particular assignment or activity fits into the teacher's overall plan, but the teacher expects students to complete the work and it is your job to see that it gets done. The fill-in activities and lessons you bring should be used only when the assigned work is completed, or the plans are unable to be carried out.

There will be situations when the teacher for some reason, cannot leave lessons plans, when the plans left are impossible to decipher, or activities are too short for the time available. These situations leave you with the challenge of filling class time with manageable and worthwhile activities of your own. Every substitute should have some tried and true activities which work without fail in their **Super SubPack**.

Visit The Professional Substitute Teacher Website and test your knowledge at:

http://subed.usu.edu

The activities and lesson ideas in this chapter are not intended to replace the lesson plans of the permanent teacher, but rather to supplement them and help provide quality learning experiences throughout the day.

Notes About Activities And Lesson Ideas

The activities and lessons in Chapter Five have been organized into the following three sections: *5-Minute Fillers*, *Early Finishers*, and *Short Activities*. Five-Minute Fillers are whole class, teacher directed activities for those few extra minutes which often occur throughout the school day. Early Finisher Activities are for when individual students finish assignments early and need something constructive to do. The Short Activities section has been divided by subject content and includes lessons and activities that can be completed in 60 minutes or less.

Suggestions for Implementing Activities and Lessons

- Many of the activities and lessons in this book indicate an approximate time needed to complete the activity. However, these are guidelines only. These lessons can be adapted for grade levels other than those suggested and the time needed to complete each activity will vary with the age and ability of the students.

- Contents are arranged by topic, however, many lessons are appropriate for several different subjects. By familiarizing yourself with all of the lessons, you will be able to make the best use of everything this book has to offer.

- The worksheets and activities in this chapter are designed to stimulate thinking, provide practice in deduction, as well as to enhance the standard core curriculum. Try to convey them as an opportunity to learn something new, rather than as an evaluation of what students already know.

- Consider letting students work in groups to complete assignments, or work independently then in groups for the last five minutes. This removes some of the extreme pressure students feel to get the "right" answer.

- When using worksheets, prepare the students with a discussion or brainstorming activity before handing them out. If their minds are in gear and they are already thinking about the topic, they will learn more as they process the information on the page.

Fill-In Activities

- If you don't have the time or resources to photocopy student worksheets, consider completing them orally. Read the questions aloud and then allow students to respond. The material can be adapted to fit any time frame using this presentation style.

- Be specific in your instructions. If the assignment should be done without talking, say, "Work Silently," if it needs to be completed in 15 minutes let the students know.

- Allow enough time to check answers or share results at the end of an activity or assignment. If this is not possible, at least leave an answer key with the permanent teacher for students to check their work the next day.

- Answers for students to check their own work can be provided in a number of ways. The teacher can read them aloud at the end of the activity. An answer key can be taped to a desk or wall for students to consult, or answer keys can be photocopied and distributed when students finish the assignment.

- Always evaluate student work before returning it to them. Even just a couple of words at the top of the page, recognizes student effort, and validates the worth of the assignment.

- If you gave the assignment, it's your responsibility to correct and evaluate the students' work.

- Summarizing the activity helps to ensure that learning has taken place. One simple way to do this is to have students, or groups, take turns stating one new thing they learned from the activity.

Of Special Note

Evaluating student work validates student effort.

In many of the lessons plans which follow, the last procedure is, "*hand in work for teacher evaluation.*" It is important that you, the teacher for that lesson, note some type of evaluation on the students' papers. Often it will work out so you can evaluate and return papers to students before they go home. Other times it may take a few minutes after school to make a note on the papers and leave them for the permanent teacher to distribute. In either case it is important that *you*, the teacher who assigned the work, be the one to evaluate it. This validates the students' work and helps them feel like the assignment had a purpose. If you simply leave the papers for the permanent teacher they will probably be either handed back without an evaluation or perhaps even thrown away. In either case, the students will come to believe that assignments they do with a substitute teacher are not really important because no one took the time to look at their work and comment about it. A stamp, a sticker, or a few positive words at the top of the page is all it takes to make students feel good about their efforts.

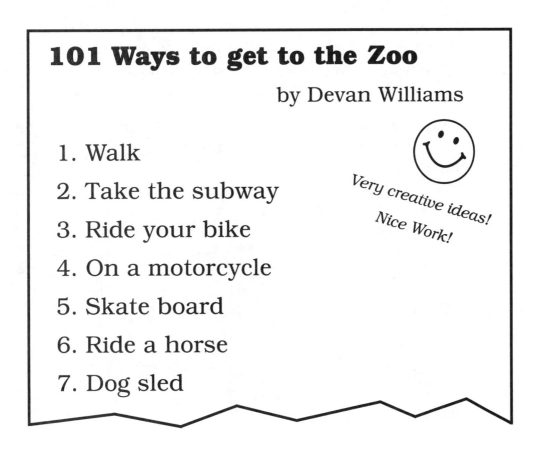

101 Ways to get to the Zoo

by Devan Williams

1. Walk

2. Take the subway

3. Ride your bike

4. On a motorcycle

5. Skate board

6. Ride a horse

7. Dog sled

Very creative ideas! Nice Work!

Table of Contents for Activities

Chapter Five: Activities and Lessons

5-Minute Fillers

Introduction:

This section contains critical thinking activities designed to keep the whole class attentive and involved during those last five minutes before lunch, to get everyone re-focused after recess, or at any other odd moments that occur throughout the day.

Grades K-5

If I Were A . . .

This activity can be done while students are sitting in their desks or waiting in a line. Begin by saying, "If I were a . . ." Have one student name a general topic such as food, sport, plant, animal, etc. Give each student a chance to finish the statement while the rest of the class listens.

Example: "If I were a food, I would be a pizza."

Grades 3-8

Brain Teasers and Riddles

1. What is full of holes, yet holds water? **A sponge**

2. What is bought by the yard, yet worn by the foot? **Carpet**

3. What is the longest word in the English language? **Smiles. There is a mile between the first and last letter.**

4. If eight birds are on a roof and you shoot at one, how many remain? **None. They all fly away.**

5. Why can't it rain for two days continually? **Because there is always a night in between.**

6. What speaks every language? **An echo**

7. Why is a nose in the middle of a face? **Because it is the scenter.**

8. What table is completely without legs? **A time-table**

9. What is the difference between a jeweler and a jailer? **One sells watches, the other watches cells.**

10. What is black and white and read all over? **A newspaper.**

11. Can a man living in Chicago be buried west of the Mississippi? **No. He is still alive.**

12. How far can a dog run into the woods? **Halfway. The other half he is running out.**

13. A farmer had seventeen sheep. All but nine died. How many did he have left? **Nine.**

14. A man has two coins in his hand. The two coins total thirty cents. One is not a nickel. What are the two coins? **A nickel and a quarter. (The other is a nickel.)**

15. How many animals of each species did Moses take aboard the Ark? **None. (it was Noah)**

Minute Mysteries

Grades 3-8

"Minute Mysteries" are stories that are told within a minute and then require the listeners to solve a mystery. Students generate questions that can be answered with a simple "yes" or "no" in order to solve the mystery. These stories are fun and teach children to use critical thinking skills while they sort through the information to figure out the answer.

1. A cowboy left town on Tuesday and was gone three days, coming back on Tuesday.

    Q. *How is that possible?*

    A. **His horse was named Tuesday.**

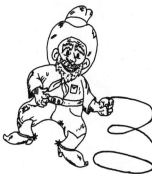

2. A man is found dead in a cabin in the ocean.

    Q. *What could have happened?*

    A. **The man is in the cabin of an airplane which crashed in the ocean.**

3. A person lived on the 15th floor of a high-rise apartment building. Everyday he got on the elevator, rode down to the lobby and went to work. Every evening he came home from work, rode the elevator to the 13th floor and walked up the stairs to his apartment.

Q   Why?

A.   The person is very short and can only reach the elevator button to the 13th floor.

4.   A man was lonely and wanted a talking parrot to keep him company. He went to the pet store and found a beautiful bird that was for sale at a bargain price. He asked the store owner if the bird could be trained to talk. The owner said, *"This bird is absolutely guaranteed to repeat everything it hears."* So the man bought the bird and took it home. But two weeks later he returned to the store, demanding his money back, saying, *"The bird refused to talk."* The store owner said, *"I stand by my guarantee and will not give your money back."*

Q.   How could he say that, considering the bird wouldn't talk?

A.   The parrot was deaf.

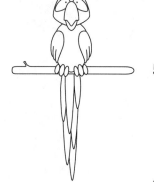

5.   A man found a hole in his suit and subsequently died.

Q.   Why?

A.   The man was an astronaut on a space walk outside his space craft.

6.   A company night watchman phoned his boss warning him not to take a business trip saying, *"Last night I dreamed that you were killed in an accident on this trip. Please don't go."* After thanking him for the warning, the boss fired him.

Q.   Why?

A.   He had been sleeping on the job.

SILLY STORY

Directions: Ask a student for the kind of word indicated. Write the word on the space provided. Repeat the process until all the spaces are filled. Read the completed **Silly Story** aloud to the class.

Getting to School

You would not believe the (1) _____ time I had getting to school today. First of all my alarm went off at (2) _____ a.m. instead of (3) _____ a.m., which is the time I usually get up. When I (4)_____ my closet to decide what to wear the only clothes I could find were (5) _____ (6) _____ and (7) _____ (8) _____. Luckily the outfit I'd been wearing for the past (9) _____ days was still in the laundry basket so I put it on. Then I went to the (10) _____ to eat breakfast but, the only food I could find was (11) _____ and week old (12) _____ so I (13) _____ them together and ate it (14) _____. As if that wasn't bad enough, when I went to brush my teeth (15) _____ came out of the faucet instead of water. I was not having a (16) _____ day. Then my (17) _____ couldn't find the (18) _____ to the car, so I had to walk all the way to school carrying the (19) _____ (20) _____ I had made for my (21) _____ class project. Halfway to school a (22) _____ started chasing me so I (23) _____ ran the rest of the way. I rushed inside the front (24) _____ just as the late bell rang. I sure do hope the rest of my day goes (25) _____.

1.	adjective	14.	adverb ending in "ly"
2.	time	15.	liquid
3.	time	16.	adjective
4.	past tense verb	17.	member of a family
5.	color	18.	part of a car
6.	piece of clothing	19.	adjective
7.	adjective	20.	noun
8.	piece of clothing	21.	school subject
9.	number	22.	animal
10.	room in a house	23.	adverb ending in "ly"
11.	food	24.	part of a building
12.	food	25.	adverb
13.	past tense verb		

* Additional Silly Stories can be found in the *Language Arts* section on page186.

Mind Benders

1. The Shopping Trip

One day last week my brother went to town with only $10 in his pocket, but returned in the evening with $20.

He bought a pair of shoes at Chipmans and some meat at the meat market. He also had his eyes examined. It so happens that my brother gets paid every Thursday by check and the banks in this town are open on Tuesday, Friday, and Saturday only. The eye doctor is not in his office on Saturday and there is no market on Thursday or Friday. What day did my brother go to town?

2. The Chess Tournament Dilemma

Four men named P.F. Smith, C.J. Smith, Reynolds, and Fellows played in a chess tournament.

The Smiths were the famous Smith brothers, twins who played opposite ends on the Princeton football team.

Reynolds surprised everyone when he defeated Fellows.

The man who finished third said graciously to the winner at the conclusion of the matches, "I've heard a great deal about you and I am happy to meet you. May I congratulate you."

The runner-up was terribly crippled, having had infantile paralysis when he was four years old. As a result he had never married, but had lived a sheltered life with his widowed mother, making chess his chief diversion.

P.F. Smith sometimes talked too much. He had disgraced himself when he was an usher at Fellow's wedding by making the bride's mother late to the wedding.

In what order did the men finish?

3. The Artisans

There are three men, named James, John, and Jake, each of whom is engaged in two occupations. Their occupations classify each of them as two of the following: chauffeur, electrician, musician, painter, gardener, and barber. From the following facts, find in what two occupations each man is engaged.

1. The chauffeur offended the musician by laughing at his long hair.
2. Both the musician and the gardener used to go fishing with James.
3. The painter had the electrician wire his new house.
4. The chauffeur dated the painter's sister.
5. John owed the gardener $5.00.
6. Jake beat both John and the painter at horse shoes.

4. The Stolen Antique

Three men, Mr. White, Mr. Black and Mr. Brown and their wives were entertained at the home of their friend one evening. After the departure of the guests, the host and hostess discovered that a valuable antique had been stolen. It was later discovered that one of the six guests was the thief. From the facts given, see if you can discover who it was.

1. The spouse of the thief lost money at cards that evening.
2. Because of partial paralysis of his hands and arms, Mr. Brown was unable to drive his car.
3. Mrs. Black and another female guest spent the entire evening doing a jigsaw puzzle.
4. Mr. Black accidentally spilled a drink on Mrs. White when he was introduced to her.
5. Mr. Brown gave his wife half of the money that he had won to make up for her loss.
6. Mr. Black had beaten the thief in golf that day.

Solutions to Mind Benders:

1. **The Shopping Trip**
   My brother went to town on Tuesday.

2. **Chess Tournament Dilemma**
   Winner-C.J. Smith
   Runner-up- Reynolds
   Third- Fellows
   Fourth- P.F. Smith

3. **The Artisans**
   James- barber and painter
   John- musician and electrician
   Jake- chauffeur and gardener

4. **The Stolen Antique**
   Mrs. Black was the thief.

Mystery Box

**Grades
K-8**

Place an object in a box or sack. Ask the students how they can find out what is in the box without looking at it. Allow them to shake the box, smell the box, and feel its weight.

Suggest playing a version of "20 questions," asking questions that require a "yes" or "no" answer to figure out what is in the box. If students ask a lot of random questions, encourage them to eliminate categories. Questions such as, "Is it something that would be used in the kitchen?" or "Is it something that would be purchased at a sporting goods store?" can cover a lot of items quickly. When students guess the object in the box, take it out and show it to them. Variations on mystery boxes are a lot of fun and are excellent "time fillers" that develop good thinking skills.

Word Puzzles

**Grades
4-8**

Copy the Word Puzzles below on the chalk board and have students guess the phrases they represent.

SAND	N E V E S	cycle cycle cycle	little little late late	**BLOOD** WATER

Answers: *sand box, seven-up, tricycle, too little too late, and blood is thicker than water*

* Additional word puzzles can be found on pages 138 and 139.

Number Phrases

Grades 4-8

Copy one or more of the abbreviated phrases below on the board, then challenge students to guess the phrase. (see answers below)

A. 26 - L. of the A.

B. 7 - W. of the W.

C. 54 - C. in a D. (with the J.)

D. 88 - P. K.

E. 18 - H. on a G. C.

F. 90 - D. in a R. A.

G. 4 - Q. in a G.

H. 24 - H. in a D.

I. 11 - P. on a F. T.

J. 29 - D. in F. in a L. Y.

K. 76 - T. L. the B. P.

L. 20,000 - L. U. T. S.

M. 7 - D. of the W.

N. 12 - E. in a D.

O. 3 - B. M. (S. H. T. R.!)

ANSWERS:

A. 26 letters of the alphabet

B. 7 wonders of the world

C. 54 cards in a deck (with the Joker)

D. 88 piano keys

E. 18 holes on a golf course

F. 90 degrees in a right angle

G. 4 quarts in a gallon

H. 24 hours in a day

I. 11 players on a football team

J. 29 days in February in a Leap Year

K. 76 trombones lead the big parade

L. 20,000 leagues under the sea

M. 7 days of the week

N. 12 eggs in a dozen

O. 3 blind mice (see how they run!)

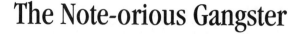

The Note-orious Gangster

Coded note

As a general rule, the big shots of the underworld do not go in for music. Perhaps that is why, last February, Detective Duke overlooked the meaning in this apparently harmless note.

If you read it, you will readily see that it is nothing more than a rough draft of an election speech and certainly has no connection with crime. *But why the musical notes at the top?*

Close examination and careful study of this note reveals an important message and had the police been able to read between the lines they would have prevented one of the biggest robberies in recent years.

What can YOU make of this message?

Solution: If you can read music, the solution is simple. Read the notes and write them in the order they appear. Now, go to the message and read until you find a word that begins with the first letter, "b". The word is "be". Start reading again and stop at the first word beginning with an "a", which is "at". Continue again until you come to a "c" word, "citizens". The message reads: **Be at Citizens Bank Friday at five. Easy cleanup for fifty grand.**

The Plimpton Hold Up

If you were present for three minutes at the scene of the hold up pictured below and later were questioned as a witness, how many questions relating to it could you answer? Study this picture carefully for three minutes and without referring to the picture again, answer as many of the questions as you can.

The Plimpton Hold Up Questions

1. In what town did the hold-up occur?

2. What was held up?

3. What is its correct address?

4. On the corner of what two streets is it?

5. Is the thief in the picture?

6. Where is he?

7. How much money did he steal?

8. Did the policeman see the hold-up?

9. What is he doing about it?

10. What is the name of the taxi company?

11. What is the number of the taxi?

12. In what direction is the taxi going?

13. What time did the hold-up take place?

14. What is the date?

15. How many people are shown?

16. How many are aware of the hold-up?

17. What kind of store is next to the bank?

18. Who owns it?

19. What is its correct address?

20. What kind of store is on the corner?

21. Who owns it?

22. What is the number of this store?

23. At the intersection of what two streets is it?

24. Which of these two is the one-way street?

25. In what direction does traffic go on this street?

26. Where is the hydrant?

27. What does the sign on 20th Street advertise?

28. What is the price of the advertised product?

29. Is there a mailbox shown?

30. On what street are the car tracks?

Other 5-Minute Filler Ideas

Early Finishers

In every class, every day, there will be several students who finish their assignments early. With nothing to do, even "good" students will often behave inappropriately and disrupt the work of the whole class. The following activities are designed to keep *early finishers* involved in constructive activities that won't disrupt the rest of the class. They also provide great motivation for students to work hard, and finish their assignments so they can participate in these fun activities.

At The Back Of The Room:

- Set up a puzzle that students can work on throughout the day.

- Set up a reading corner where students can go and read silently after they have finished an assignment.

- Tangram puzzles (see page 158).

Activity Pages:

Copy some of the activities in this section to keep in your **Super SubPack**. At the beginning of the day explain that these fun worksheets will be available for students who finish assignments early throughout the day. You may want to set out a couple of different sheets and let students choose which ones they would like to do. Be prepared with enough worksheets for each student in the class to have one, because students who don't get to do them in class will often want to take one home to do "just for fun." As you leave the school at the end of the day, ask if you can make copies to replace those the students used.

Things I Like To . . .

TOUCH

SMELL

SEE

HEAR

TASTE

Name _____

Color Me Page

Substitute Teaching Institute/Utah State University

NAME _____

Color Me Page

©Substitute Teaching Institute/Utah State University

Dot Design

Copy each design on the blank grid.

1.

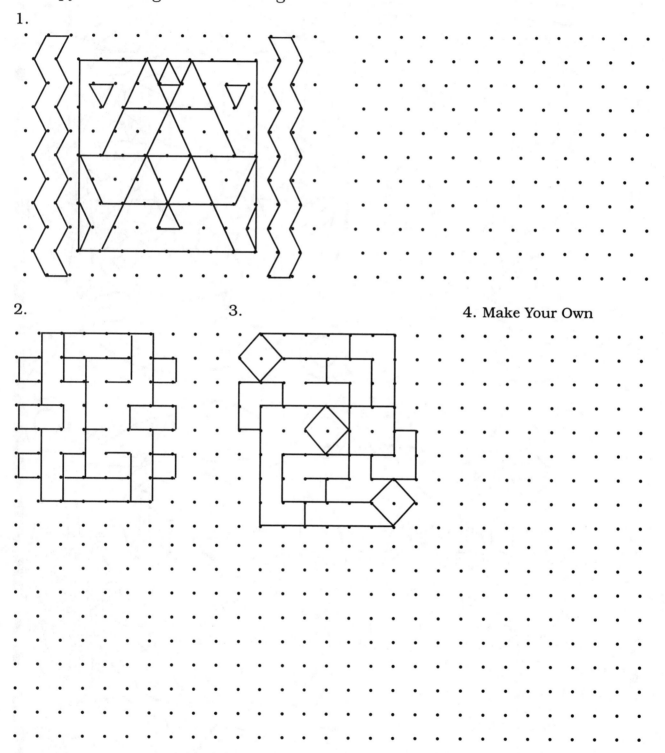

2.   3.   4. Make Your Own

All About Me

1. Draw a picture of your family.

2. Write the names of four friends in your class.

3. Draw three clocks. Show:
    A) when you got up.
    B) when you eat lunch.
    C) when you go to bed.

4. Draw a car using only circles.

5. Write the numbers counting by 5's to 50.

6. Write a sentence using six words that start with the letter B.

7. Make a list of everything you ate yesterday.

8. Close your eyes. Listen! Write down six things you hear.

9. What is your favorite color? List 5 things that color.

10. Write down 10 things you would like to get for your birthday.

11. If you were the teacher what would you do?

12. Write the numbers backwards from 25 to 0.

13. Write down 7 things that start with the same letter as your first name.

14. Draw an animal using only triangles.

15. Write down 5 things you will use today that start with the letter T.

16. How old are you?

17. If you smiled at everyone you saw for one whole day, what do you think would happen?

18. Write the days of the week.

19. What is your favorite animal?

20. If you could do anything you wanted, what would you do today?

Brr. . . . Can you ~~selbrmacnu~~ unscramble these cold words?

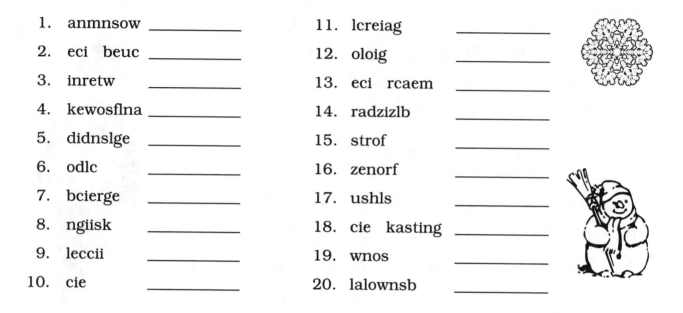

1. anmnsow _____
2. eci beuc _____
3. inretw _____
4. kewosflna _____
5. didnslge _____
6. odlc _____
7. bcierge _____
8. ngiisk _____
9. leccii _____
10. cie _____

11. lcreiag _____
12. oloig _____
13. eci rcaem _____
14. radzizlb _____
15. strof _____
16. zenorf _____
17. ushls _____
18. cie kasting _____
19. wnos _____
20. lalownsb _____

How many words can you think of that end in "ice" **There are at least 75!**

_____
_____
_____
_____
_____
_____
_____
_____
_____
_____
_____
_____
_____
_____
_____

Answers found at the end of this section.

Weather Words

If you can unscramble these weather words, then you're hot stuff!

1. nira   _____
2. hsnusnie   _____
3. ucloyd   _____
4. fownaslke   _____
5. ouownpdr   _____
6. nynsu   _____
7. dunhtre   _____
8. doanort   _____
9. ryd   _____
10. zaribdlz   _____
11. locd   _____
12. morthmerete   _____
13. yic   _____
14. zidzrel   _____
15. emarptreuet   _____

16. taterpoincpii _____
17. mwra   _____
18. owrinab   _____
19. idmuh   _____
20. hgignnlit   _____
21. etw   _____
22. toh   _____
23. ndywi   _____
24. aifanllr   _____
25. gogfy   _____
26. stacvoer   _____
27. wnos   _____
28. stacrefo   _____
29. ialh   _____
30. morts   _____

Answers found at the end of this section.

Alphabet Soup

Insert a letter of the alphabet into each of the twenty-six empty boxes to complete a word reading across. The missing letter you add may occur any place in the word. Each letter of the alphabet is used only once. Cross off the letters as you use them. The first line has been completed for you.

A B ~~C~~ D ~~E~~ F ~~G~~ H ~~I~~ J K ~~L~~ ~~M~~ N ~~O~~ P ~~Q~~ ~~R~~ S T U V W X Y Z

B	I	C	E	C	R	E	A	M	L	T	E
T	E	D	D	Y		E	A	R	P	O	S
R	C	G	P	U		Z	L	E	A	U	J
S	K	I	V	P		U	A	R	T	E	R
I	L	H	J	U		G	L	E	C	X	P
O	K	J	U	M		R	O	P	E	A	Y
T	X	O	B	E		L	O	W	E	R	G
F	D	A	D	O		R	T	I	J	H	Q
K	N	X	E	C		A	I	R	O	V	F
Y	G	F	C	R		Y	O	N	T	P	C
L	U	R	A	I		C	O	A	T	H	G
Z	P	O	N	B		C	Y	C	L	E	V
O	L	Q	R	E		T	R	O	P	L	D
D	I	B	K	U		E	W	E	L	K	B
K	T	Y	M	U		M	Y	U	X	E	R
L	S	X	W	A		C	H	I	U	K	B
G	E	O	R	O		K	E	T	F	F	S
C	Y	B	U	C		E	T	N	T	H	U
I	H	P	O	P		D	D	L	E	K	L
R	O	G	A	R		E	N	S	E	M	A
R	Y	S	O	L		E	S	O	H	J	L
X	T	E	N	B		A	N	K	E	T	O
P	B	V	I	S		E	A	T	E	R	F
K	M	C	X	Y		L	L	O	W	I	Y
I	K	U	G	L		G	F	V	C	I	M
M	N	M	C	E		C	I	T	E	D	P

Answers found at the end of this section.

Substitute Teaching Institute/Utah State University

Let's Play Baseball

Use the following clues to help you identify 25 words associated with the game of baseball.

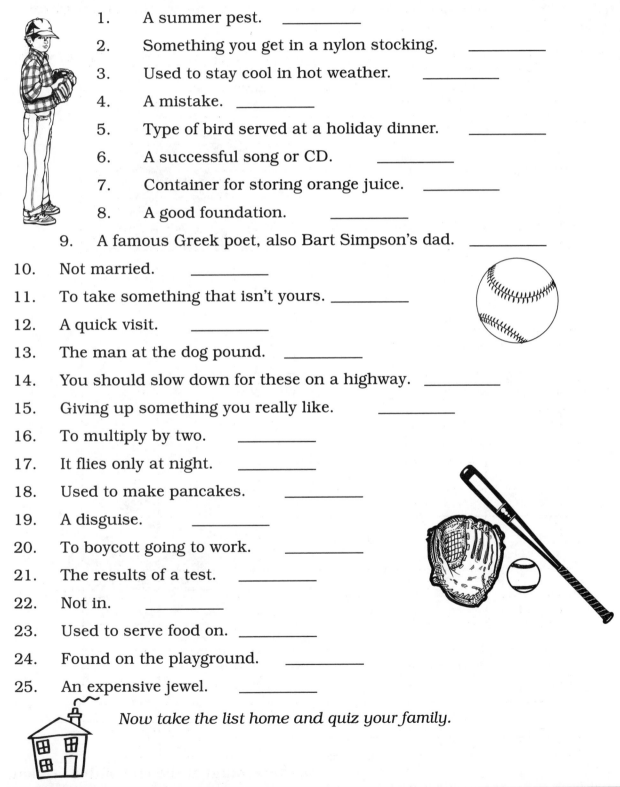

1. A summer pest. _____
2. Something you get in a nylon stocking. _____
3. Used to stay cool in hot weather. _____
4. A mistake. _____
5. Type of bird served at a holiday dinner. _____
6. A successful song or CD. _____
7. Container for storing orange juice. _____
8. A good foundation. _____
9. A famous Greek poet, also Bart Simpson's dad. _____
10. Not married. _____
11. To take something that isn't yours. _____
12. A quick visit. _____
13. The man at the dog pound. _____
14. You should slow down for these on a highway. _____
15. Giving up something you really like. _____
16. To multiply by two. _____
17. It flies only at night. _____
18. Used to make pancakes. _____
19. A disguise. _____
20. To boycott going to work. _____
21. The results of a test. _____
22. Not in. _____
23. Used to serve food on. _____
24. Found on the playground. _____
25. An expensive jewel. _____

Now take the list home and quiz your family.

Food Cryptograms

A cryptogram is a coded word. Can you crack the code and figure out the words?
All of the cryptograms below are kinds of food. The first word has been done for
you; it will help you decode the others.

s	p	a	g	h	e	t	t	i
v	h	f	m	r	k	n	n	w

___	___	___	___	___
h	w	a	a	f

___	___	___	___	___	___	___	___
w	e	k	e	j	k	f	y

___	___	___	___	___	___	___	___	___
r	f	y	d	o	j	m	k	j

___	___	___	___	___	___	___	___	___	___	___
l	j	k	z	e	r	l	j	w	k	v

___	___	___	___	___	___
s	j	f	z	m	k

___	___	___	___	___	___	___
h	s	h	i	s	j	z

___	___	___	___	___	___
e	f	j	j	s	n

___	___	___	___	___	___	___	___	___
m	j	f	h	k	l	j	o	w	n

___	___	___	___	___	___	___
e	o	e	o	y	d	k	j

Answers found at the end of this section.

Substitute Teaching Institute/Utah State University

Sports Cryptograms

A cryptogram is a coded word. Can you crack the code and figure out the words? All of the cryptograms below are sports. The first word has been done for you; it will help you decode the others.

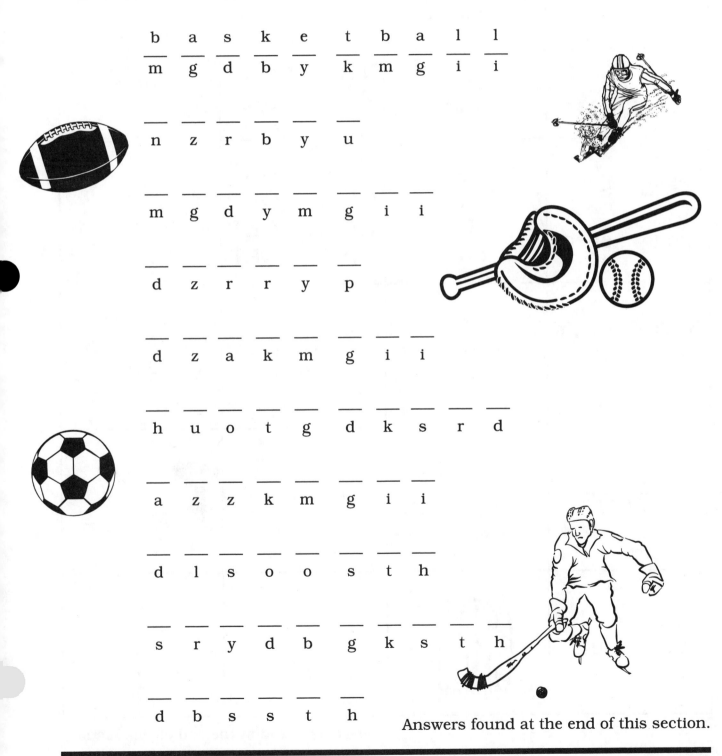

b a s k e t b a l l
m g d b y k m g i i

___ ___ ___ ___ ___ ___
n z r b y u

___ ___ ___ ___ ___ ___ ___ ___
m g d y m g i i

___ ___ ___ ___ ___ ___
d z r r y p

___ ___ ___ ___ ___ ___ ___
d z a k m g i i

___ ___ ___ ___ ___ ___ ___ ___ ___
h u o t g d k s r d

___ ___ ___ ___ ___ ___ ___
a z z k m g i i

___ ___ ___ ___ ___ ___ ___
d l s o o s t h

___ ___ ___ ___ ___ ___ ___ ___
s r y d b g k s t h

___ ___ ___ ___ ___ ___
d b s s t h

Answers found at the end of this section.

©Substitute Teaching Institute/Utah State University

Word Puzzles I

Directions:

These puzzles represent common expressions and phrases. Solve them by carefully noticing the positions of the words and letters. Are they under, over, mixed-up, inside, or a certain size?

E K A KISSM	search and	NEFRIENDED	$\dfrac{\text{wear}}{\text{long}}$
egsg gesg segg sgeg	S M O K E	GIVE GET GIVE GET GIVE GET GIVE GET	$\dfrac{\text{cover}}{\text{agent}}$
NOT GUILTY STANDER	$\dfrac{\text{man}}{\text{board}}$	$\dfrac{\text{EZ}}{\text{iiii}}$	LM AL EA AE EM ML
$\dfrac{\text{BELT}}{\text{HITTING}}$	A D S L A	he ⟩ art	**T.V.**
ar up ms	**CHAIR**	TIRE	T O W N

Answers found at the end of this section.

Word Puzzles II

Directions:

These puzzles represent common expressions and phrases. Solve them by carefully noticing the positions of the words and letters. Are they under, over, mixed-up, inside, or a certain size?

I [SOCK]	1,000, **1**000	C O S T S (scattered)	ground feet feet feet feet feet feet
g o i g n (circle) a r o d u n (circle)	time time	stand I	T O U C H
FRIENDS standing/miss FRIENDS	WALKING	SOUP	ter very esting
r|e|a|d|i|n|g	b sick ed	LO head/heels VE	knee lights
g r u the block n i n n	every|right|thing	R R O O A D D S S	i/8

Answers found at the end of this section.

©Substitute Teaching Institute/Utah State University

How Well Can You
Follow Directions?

Start in the United States and follow the directions to see where you end up.

1. Write down: THE UNITED STATES OF AMERICA

2. Take out all of the E's.

3. Take out every fifth letter.

4. Change the F to an A.

5. Move the S's to the front of the word.

6. Take out all of the T's.

7. Take out the first vowel and the last consonant.

8. Move the fourth and fifth letter to the end of the word.

9. Replace the S's with L's.

10. Remove the sixth, seventh, and eighth letters.

11. Move the double L's to be the third and fourth letters.

12. Where did you end up? _____

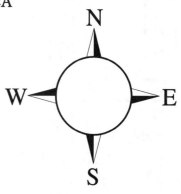

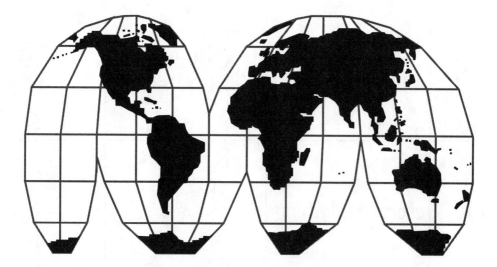

Answer found at the end of this section.

Substitute Teaching Institute/Utah State University

Answers To Early Finisher Activities

Cold Scrambled Words:

1. snow man
2. ice cube
3. winter
4. snowflake
5. sledding
6. cold
7. iceberg
8. skiing
9. icicle
10. ice
11. glacier
12. igloo
13. ice cream
14. blizzard
15. frost
16. frozen
17. slush
18. ice skating
19. snow
20. snowball

Weather Words:

1. rain
2. sunshine
3. cloudy
4. snowflake
5. downpour
6. sunny
7. thunder
8. tornado
9. dry
10. blizzard
11. cold
12. thermometer
13. icy
14. drizzle
15. temperature
16. precipitation
17. warm
18. rainbow
19. humid
20. lightning
21. wet
22. hot
23. windy
24. rainfall
25. foggy
26. overcast
27. snow
28. forecast
29. hail
30. storm

Alphabet Soup:

1. ice cream
2. teddy bear
3. puzzle
4. quarter
5. juggle
6. jump rope
7. flower
8. door
9. chair
10. crayon
11. raincoat
12. bicycle
13. rest
14. jewel
15. mummy
16. watch
17. rocket
18. bucket
19. puddle
20. garden
21. solve
22. blanket
23. sweater
24. yellow
25. ugly
26. excited

Baseball:

1. fly
2. run
3. fan
4. error
5. foul (fowl)
6. hit
7. pitcher
8. base
9. homer
10. single
11. steal
12. short stop
13. catcher
14. curve
15. sacrifice
16. double
17. bat
18. batter
19. mask
20. strike
21. score
22. out
23. plate
24. swing/slide
25. diamond

Food Cryptograms:

1. spaghetti
2. pizza
3. ice cream
4. hamburger
5. french fries
6. orange
7. popcorn
8. carrot
9. grapefruit
10. cucumber

Sports Cryptograms:

1. basketball
2. hockey
3. baseball
4. soccer
5. softball
6. gymnastics
7. football
8. swimming
9. ice skating
10. skiing

Word Puzzles I:

1. kiss and make up
2. search high and low
3. friend in need
4. long underwear
5. scrambled eggs
6. up in smoke
7. forgive and forget
8. undercover agent
9. innocent bystander
10. man overboard
11. easy on the eyes
12. three square meals
13. hitting below the belt
14. tossed salad
15. broken heart
16. black and white TV
17. up in arms
18. high chair
19. flat tire
20. downtown

Word Puzzles II:

1. sock in the eye
2. one in a million
3. rising costs
4. six feet underground
5. going around in circles
6. time after time
7. I understand
8. touchdown
9. mis-understanding between friends
10. walking tall
11. split pea soup
12. very interesting
13. reading between the lines
14. sick in bed
15. head over heals in love
16. neon lights
17. running around the block
18. right in the middle of everything
19. cross roads
20. I over ate

Following Directions:

Answer: *Holland*

Short Activities and Lessons:

The activities and lessons in the following section have been developed for whole class, teacher directed instruction. The section is organized according to subject and each type of lesson is easily identified by the corresponding icon shown below. Within each subject there are activities for every grade level.

Critical

Thinking

Math

Science

Geo Art Gallery

Subject: Art

Grade: K-8

Time: 30 minutes

Materials Needed:

Several sets of tangrams (ideally one set for each student). These can either be purchased commercially or made using colored card stock and the templates found at the end of this lesson. (See page 146.)

Advance Preparation:

Objective:

Students will use basic geometric shapes to create a work of art.

Procedure:

1. Divide the class into six groups.

2. Show the class the tangram pieces and explain that they will be using these colored geometric shapes to create a work of art.

3. Stress that any student who behaves inappropriately (i.e. throwing the tangram pieces) will be removed from his or her group and not be allowed to participate in the activity.

4. Allow students to decide if their group wants to work together and use all of the pieces in one big design, or divide the pieces up and make individual designs.

5. Tell the students how much time they will have to create their masterpiece. This will vary depending on the situation but try to allow at least 10 minutes.

6. Distribute tangram sets to each group. Try not to give any group two sets of the same color.

7. Have students begin working. Provide updates on how much time is left.

8. When the allotted time is up explain that they will spend the last five minutes of the lesson touring the "classroom gallery" and seeing the work of other artists.

9. When touring time is finished have students separate the pieces back into the original tangram sets. (If each set is a different color this process is a lot easier!). Ask one student from each group to collect the tangrams and return them to the teacher.

Extension:

Have the students make an artist information card to be displayed by their work. Things to put on the card may include the names of the artists, the number of each color used, the number of each shape used, the total number of pieces used, and a name for the work of art.

Notes For The Teacher:

Classroom management may get a little hectic during the "touring" portion of the lesson. Here are some suggestions of things to do before the tour begins to help keep things under control.

1. Review classroom rules.

2. State the expected student behavior (walking, whispering, look but don't touch, etc.).

3. Ask if anyone in the class has ever been to an art gallery or museum. Discuss the atmosphere and behavior that they observed there.

4. Compare the touring time to a trip to the library or school media center.

Notes About Tangrams

Used in the Geo-Art Gallery Activity page 144,
Tangram Puzzles page 158, and Tangram Stories page 195.

If you want to purchase commercial tangrams they are available through several school supply companies at costs between $1.00-$2.00 per set (remember that ideally each student will have their own set). Listed below are several companies with the telephone numbers for requesting a copy of their catalog.

- Summit Learning   1-800-500-8817
- Delta Education   1-800-442-5444
- Cuisenaire   1-800-237-3142

These companies also sell numerous activity packets for use with tangrams as well as many other educational materials.

If you choose to make your own tangrams here are a few suggestions:

1. Copy tangrams onto **DIFFERENT COLORS** of **HEAVY** card stock.

2. Be sure the template sheet is flat against the copier, otherwise the shapes will be distorted and not fit together properly.

3. Laminate the sheets of printed card stock before cutting the shapes apart.

4. Take the copied, laminated sheets, along with a few extra pair of scissors to school with you and let students, who finish early, cut them apart. Another option is to turn it into a class project. Have students cut them apart and then experiment making shapes while you read aloud from a good book.

5. Keep sets in sturdy zip-lock bags for storage and distribution purposes.

Purchasing or making tangrams may seem like a lot of work, but they are a versatile tool that can be used for many activities at any grade level and are well worth the effort.

Tangram Pattern

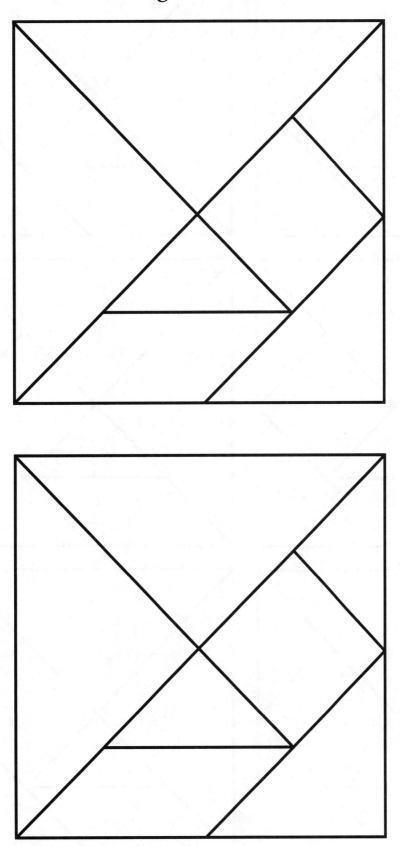

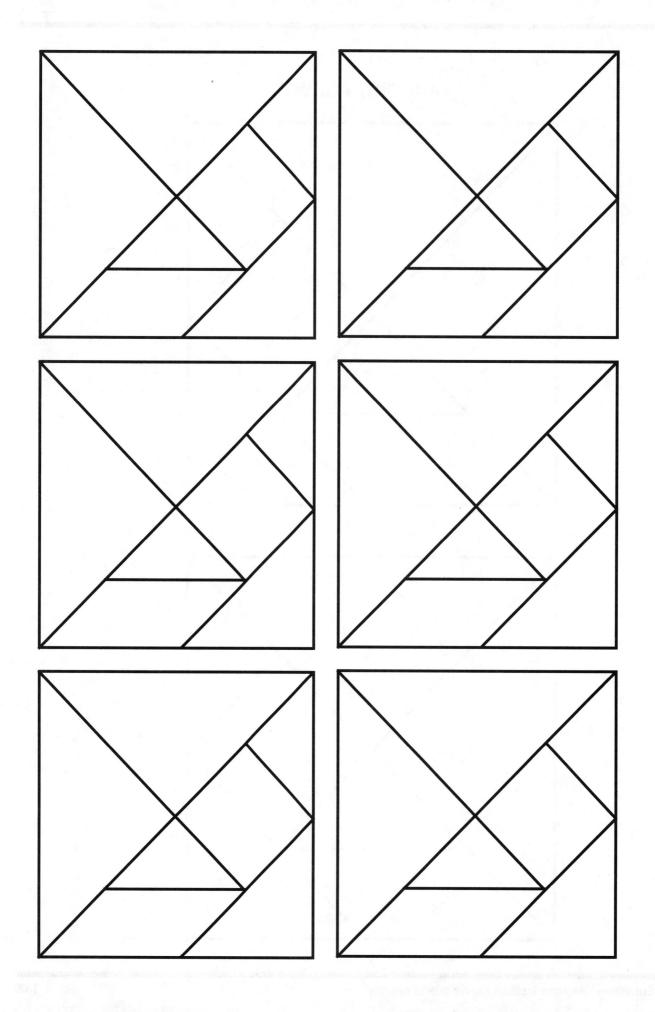

Hole Punch Art

Directions: Attach this sheet to a piece of colored paper. Use a pin or push tack to punch out the dots, then hang the colored paper up in the window!

Name _____

Hole Punch
Art

Directions: Attach this sheet to a piece of colored paper. Use a pin or push tack to punch out the dots, then hang the colored paper up in the window!

Grid Drawings

Subject: Art

Grade: 4-8

Time: 15-30 minutes

Materials Needed:

pencils, crayons, *Grid Worksheets*

Advance Preparation:

Make one copy of each worksheet for each student in the class.

Objective:

Students will use grids to help them complete or enlarge an image.

Procedure:

1. Distribute worksheets.

2. Explain directions and give helpful hints for completing the assignment. (Hints: draw in pencil first, look at the picture block by block, etc.)

3. Have students complete and color worksheets.

4. Turn in drawings for teacher evaluation.

Extension:

Collect student drawings and have students vote for their favorite. Award a prize to the class winner.

Notes For The Teacher: ————————

Students often enjoy sitting in small groups and talking quietly while they work on their drawings. If a group gets too noisy they can always be separated.

These worksheets can be copied back to back and students can choose which one they would like to complete. Students who finish early can then turn the paper over and begin working on the other activity.

You may want to create your own *Graph Art Worksheets* using holiday or lesson content themes.

Name _____

Grid Enlargement

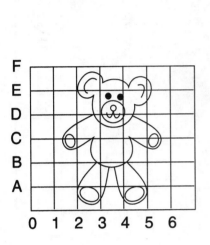

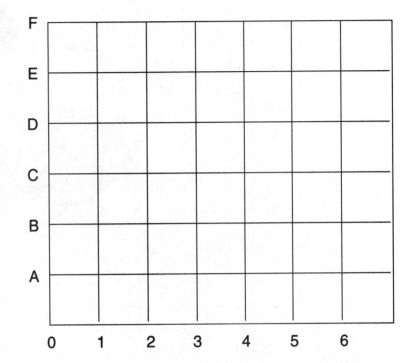

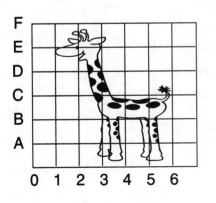

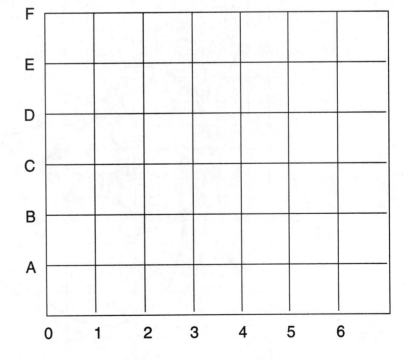

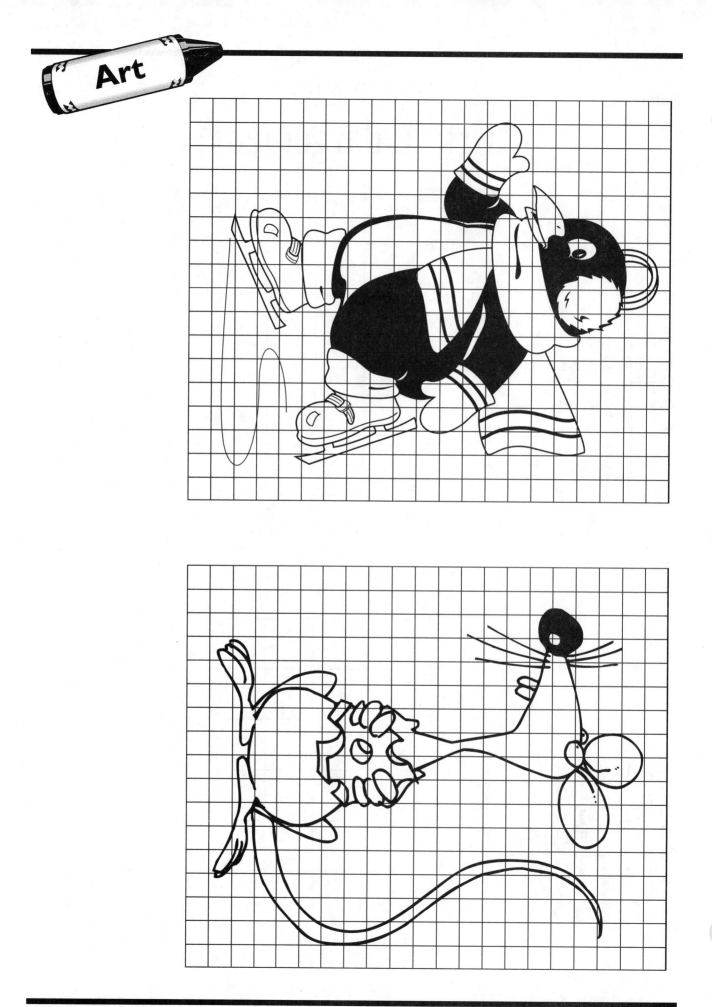

Grid Drawings

Name _____

Grid Completion

Name _____

Substitute Teaching Institute/Utah State University

Grid Completion

Name _____

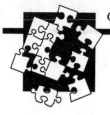

Tangram Puzzles

Subject: Critical Thinking

Grade: K-8

Time: 15-30 minutes

Materials Needed:

tangram sets (one for each student or pair of students - see Notes About Tangrams page 146)

puzzle worksheets (one for each student or pair of students)

Advance Preparation:

Photocopy puzzle worksheets

Objective:

Students will practice their spatial thinking skills.

Procedure:

1. Distribute to each student or pair of students a set of tangram pieces and copy of a tangram puzzle such as those found on page 147 and 160-161.

2. Encourage students as they rearrange the tangram pieces to construct the puzzle.

3. Students who finish early can make their own puzzles by arranging the tangram pieces on plain paper then tracing around the outside of the design. These student puzzles can be exchanged among class members.

Answers to Puzzles

Easy

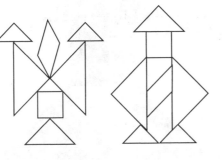

Intermediate

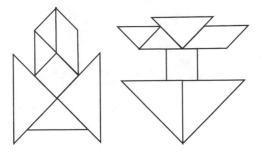

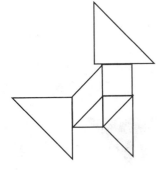 

Difficult

Notes For The Teacher:

There are many books and educational activity sets with lessons similar to *Tangram Puzzles* which can be purchased through educational supply companies. For information about requesting current catalogs see page 146.

Tangram Puzzles - Easy

Tangram Puzzles - Intermediate

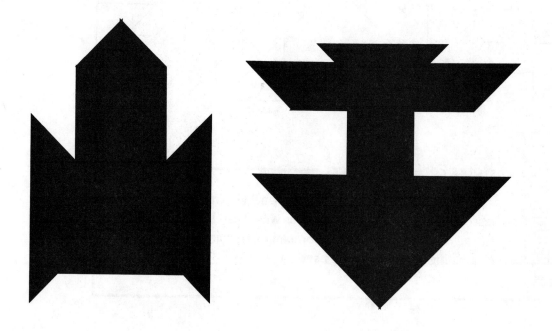

Tangram Puzzles - Difficult

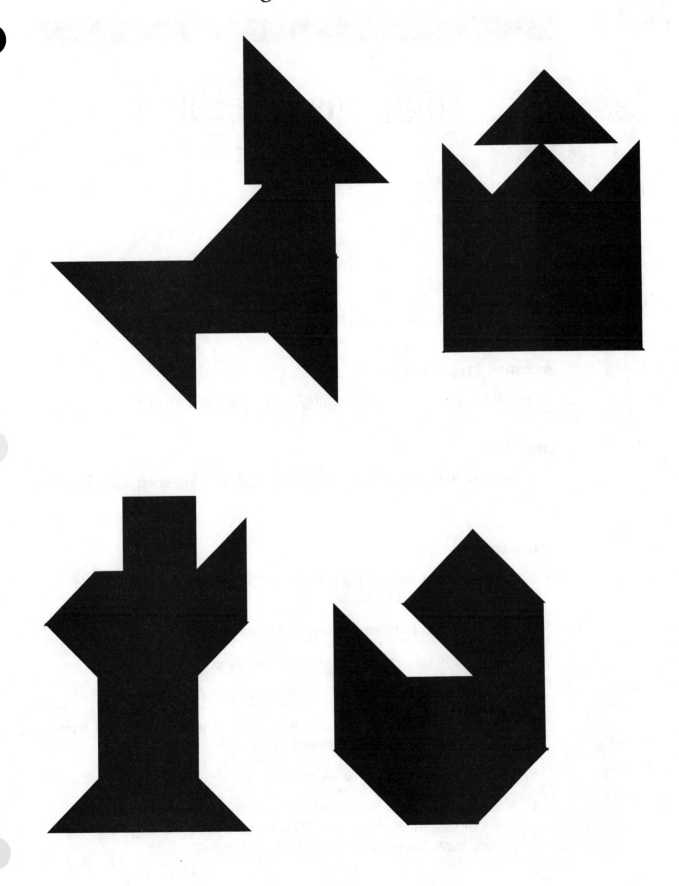

Following Directions

Subject: Critical Thinking

Grade: K-2

Time: 15-30 minutes

Materials Needed:

Teacher Data Sheet, Student Activity Sheet, crayons

Advance Preparation:

Photocopy one *Student Activity Sheet* for each student.

Objective:

Students will follow oral directions and develop their listening skills.

Procedure:

1. Ask the following questions to discuss the importance of following directions:

    1. When is it important to follow directions?

    2. Why is it important to follow directions?

    3. What could happen if you did not follow directions?

2. Hand out a worksheet to each student and have them write their names in the specified place.

3. Distribute crayons to each student.

4. Instruct the students to listen carefully as you read each set of instructions twice. Tell them not to do anything until they have listened carefully both times.

5. Read the instructions 1-5 found on the *Teacher Data Sheet*. Make sure that students do not begin until the instructions have been read twice.

6. Collect worksheets for teacher evaluation.

Extension:

Hand out blank pieces of paper and have students follow simple oral directions as the teacher gives them (i.e. put your name at the top, draw a circle in the center of the paper, make a line across the bottom of the paper, etc.).

Notes For The Teacher:

To insure that students understand the procedures and what is expected of them during this activity, quiz them about the instructions after you have explained them. Use questions such as, *"How many times will I repeat the instructions?"* and *"When do you begin following the instructions?"* to check for understanding before beginning the activity.

Teacher Data Sheet

Following Directions:

Distribute to each student a copy of the *Student Activity Sheet,* and crayons. Tell them to listen carefully while you read the instructions out loud.

Say: Listen carefully to what I say to do. I will repeat each direction only two times. Do exactly what I say.

1. Find the square with the butterfly in the corner. Put your finger on the butterfly. Color the triangle with your crayon. Put an X in the circle. Draw a circle inside of the square.

2. Find the square with the umbrella in the corner. Put your finger on the smallest square. Color the umbrella. Write the letter A in the biggest square. Draw a line through the middle square.

3. Find the square with the apple in it. Put your finger on the apple. Now look carefully at the triangle. Draw a line above the triangle. Draw a square inside the triangle. Outline the triangle with your crayon.

4. Find the square with the flower in the corner. Put your finger on the flower. Look carefully at the circles. Draw a triangle inside the top circle. Write the letter your name begins with in the biggest circle. Color the smallest circle.

5. Turn your paper over. Draw a big circle. Can you make this circle into a happy face?

Following Directions - Activity Sheet

Name _____

Guess The Object

Subject: Critical Thinking

Grade: 2-6

Time: 30+ minutes

Materials Needed:

pencil and paper

Advance Preparation:

Objective:

Students will practice their listening and oral direction skills.

Procedure:

1. Have the class draw an object as the teacher gives an oral description. The object should be simple like a toothbrush, pencil, basketball, etc.

2. Do not identify the object by name until students have had a chance to guess what it is and share their pictures with class members.

3. Repeat the activity with students giving oral directions for the class to draw and guess at.

4. Discuss the importance of listening carefully and giving good directions during this activity.

5. Discuss other situations when it is important to listen carefully or communicate clearly.

Extension:

Divide the class into teams of two and have them practice giving descriptions and listening to one another to guess what is being described.

Notes For The Teacher:

Give directions for drawing the object rather than saying it is like something else. For example, if the object was a basketball you could say, " *Draw a circle. Draw lines across it and put dots all over the inside of the circle*," rather than saying, "*It is like a baseball only bigger*."

Possible objects to describe:

Key

Baseball

Flowers

Ice Cream Cone

Umbrella

Pencil

Doodles And Directions

Subject: Critical Thinking

Grade: 2-8

Time: 30+ minutes

Materials Needed:

paper and pencil

Advance Preparation:

Procedure:

1. Have students draw a simple picture using geometric shapes (see examples). If time allows, have them color their pictures.

2. Organize the students into partners and instruct them to sit back-to-back.

3. Have one student give directions about how to draw his picture while the other follows the directions and completes a drawing on the back of his paper.

    NOTE: The student giving directions cannot look at the drawing in progress and the student drawing cannot ask questions.

4. Have the students change roles.

5. When they are finished, have the students compare pictures and discuss which directions were easy to follow and which were confusing.

Extension:

Have the students complete the activity again with a different partner. Compare the second partner's drawing with the one done by the first partner to determine which time they gave better directions.

Notes For The Teacher:

This activity can be done as a class with one student giving directions, and the other students doing the drawing at their own desks.

Examples of Geometric Shape Pictures:

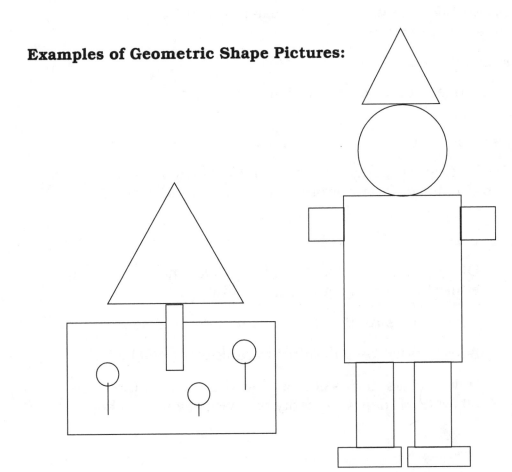

Desert Dilemma

Subject: Critical Thinking

Grade: 4-8

Time: 15-30 minutes

Materials Needed:

Desert Dilemma worksheet for each student or group

Advance Preparation:

Make photocopies of the student worksheets.

Objective:

Students will practice critical thinking skills as they analyze and discuss different priorities in a difficult situation.

Procedure:

1. Distribute to the class the *Desert Dilemma* worksheets, either individually or in small groups.

2. Review the situation and instructions as a class.

3. Allow students 10 minutes to rank the items listed.

4. Have a class discussion on how they ranked the items allowing students to justify or revise their own choices.

Extension:

Have the students list the objects on the back of their paper and put a star next to each of the objects they plan to carry. Then explain in writing how they plan to use each of these items.

Notes For The Teacher:

This is an activity where there are not necessarily right or wrong answers. It is important to establish a risk-free classroom environment where students feel comfortable sharing their ideas. Try to encourage different points of view and strongly discourage criticism of any sort.

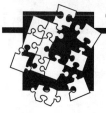

Name _____

Desert Dilemma

Situation: While driving through the desert you take a wrong turn and drive 50 miles before your car runs out of gas. You are stranded wearing shorts, a t-shirt and tennis shoes. There is nothing around you but cactus and sand. The temperature is about 110 degrees in the shade. Your only hope for rescue is to make it back to the main road.

You rummage around in the car and find the 20 items listed below. You realize that you will not be able to carry all of them with you so you rank the items according to how important you think they will be in ensuring your survival and rescue. Place the number 1 by the most important item, 2 by the second most important, and so on, with 20 being the least important item.

Remember that you are in the desert and that the three essential things for survival are food, clothing, and shelter. Work individually, and later we will discuss your choices with the rest of the class.

_____ any part of the car   _____ boots

_____ sun glasses   _____ first aid kit

_____ AM/FM radio   _____ pencil and paper

_____ blanket   _____ flash light

_____ lipstick   _____ plastic garbage bag

_____ a candy bar   _____ hammer

_____ box of matches   _____ a pack of gum

_____ silk scarf

_____ an apple

_____ a map of the state

_____ sling shot

_____ blanket

_____ 50 ft of nylon rope

Word Confetti

Subject: Critical Thinking

Grade: 4-8

Time: 15-30 minutes

Materials Needed:

pencil and paper

Advance Preparation:

Create an example of a *Word Confetti Chart* to be shared with the class as an example.

Objective:

Students will develop categorization skills.

Procedure:

1. Draw a *Word Confetti Chart* on the board or copy the sample chart found at the end of this lesson. Fill in the category row and list the words for the columns randomly around the chart.

2. As a class determine which words belong in each column and fill in the chart.

3. Have students make the outline of a Word Confetti Chart on their own paper.

4. As a class, decide on four categories and enter them in.

5. Have students independently think of four words to go into each category and write them randomly around the chart.

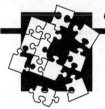

6. Exchange papers and have the students complete each other's charts.

7. Be sure the name of the person who created the chart, as well as the one who completed it, is noted on the papers and then have them turned in for teacher evaluation.

Extension:

Create another chart without listing the categories. Have the students organize the words and then write the names of the categories they have created.

Notes For The Teacher:

Start with a simple chart and obvious categories. The difficulty level of the categorization can increase once the students have mastered the mechanics of the activity.

Word Confetti Chart

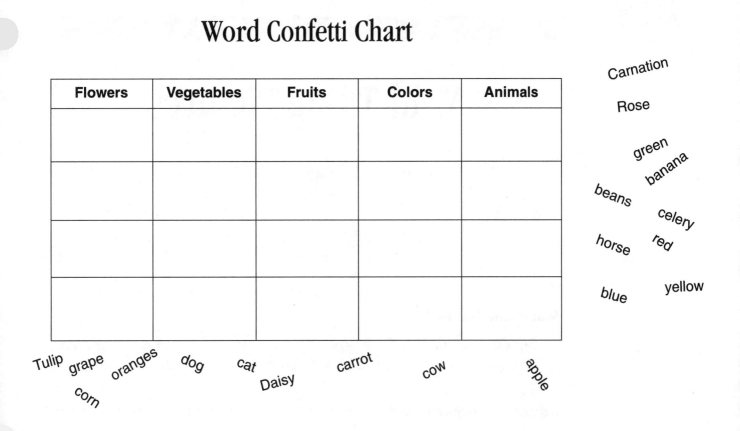

Flowers	Vegetables	Fruits	Colors	Animals

Carnation
Rose
green banana
beans celery
horse red
blue yellow

Tulip grape oranges dog cat Daisy carrot cow apple
corn

Word Confetti Chart Completed

Flowers	Vegetables	Fruits	Colors	Animals
Tulip	carrot	grape	red	horse
Daisy	beans	apple	blue	dog
Rose	corn	oranges	yellow	cow
Carnation	celery	banana	green	cat

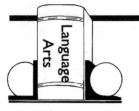

Wild Thing Pictures

Subject: Language Arts

Grade: K-3

Time: 15-30 minutes

Materials Needed:

pencils, paper, crayons, and a copy of the book *Where The Wild Things Are* by Maurice Sendak (Harper & Row Publishers)

Advance Preparation:

Cover the outside of the book so that students cannot see the author's illustrations of *wild things* as you read the story.

Objective:

Students will use their listening skills and imagination to create their own picture of a *wild thing.*

Procedure:

1. Tell the students you are going to read them a story about *wild things.*

2. Ask them to listen carefully for a description of the *wild things* so that when you are finished reading they will be able to draw a picture of one.

3. Read the story *Where The Wild Things Are* without showing any of the illustrations to the class.

4. After you have finished, ask the students to draw and color their own picture of a *wild thing.*

5. Ask volunteers to share their pictures with the class.

6. Read the story again, this time showing the author's illustrations of *wild things.*

7. Compare differences and similarities between the drawings of the author and those done by the students.

8. Collect the pictures for classroom display.

Notes For The Teacher:

Students may have difficulty recalling specific details about wild things (i.e. they live in a forest with vines, they roar, they have claws, they have yellow eyes, and terrible teeth). When this is the case it can be helpful to have a class discussion to draw out and review these details before they begin drawing.

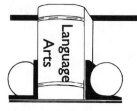

Name Poetry

Subject: Language Arts

Grade: 2-6

Time: 15-30 minutes

Materials Needed:

pencil and paper

Advance Preparation:

Create an example of a *Name Poem* to be used to teach the activity.

Objective:

Students will create a poem which is an expression of their own traits and personal characteristics.

Procedure:

1. Discuss different types of poetry. Ask students to share some poems that are familiar to them.

2. Tell the students that today they are going to create a poem about themselves.

3. Demonstrate an example of a *Name Poem* (acrostic poem) on the board.

Example:

C	is for chocolate chip cookies which are my favorite
Y	is for the yellow flowers that grow at my house
N	is for Nika my cat
T	is for the tree house I helped to build
H	is for happy thoughts
I	is for ice-cream on my birthday
A	is for all of the other things that make up me

4. Ask the students to make a name poem using their own name.

5. Share name poems with the class or in small groups.

6. Collect poems for teacher evaluation and display.

Extension:

Create *Acrostic Poems* using other topics such as holidays, school subjects, sports, etc. Illustrate the poems by drawing and coloring pictures of the things written about in the poem.

Notes For The Teacher:

Younger students may have difficulty in completing this assignment with only one example for instruction. It may be helpful to create a second poem on the board, as a class, before they write their own.

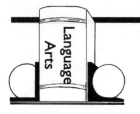

Diamente Poetry

Subject: Language Arts

Grade : 2-8

Time: 30+ minutes

Materials Needed:

pencil and paper

Advance Preparation:

Prepare a *Diamente Poem* pattern and example.

Objective:

Students will learn the Diamente Pattern for poetry and create a poem using this pattern.

Procedure:

1. Talk about a specific topic (holiday, school subject, kind of food, famous person, etc.).

2. Draw a chart on the board with the following categories: Smells, Tastes, Sounds, Sights, and Feelings.

3. Fill in the chart with student suggestions for each category.

4. Tell the students they will now use this information to write a diamente poem about this topic.

5. Explain the pattern and put it on the board. See example.

PATTERN	**EXAMPLE**
Line 1 subject	Fourth of July
Line 2 two adjectives or words that describe the subject	Fire Crackers, Bands
Line 3 three words that show action, usually "ing" words	Marching, Fighting, Picnicking
Line 4 two words that describe the subject	Flags, Sparklers
Line 5 a synonym (other name) for the subject	Independence Day

6. As a class, compose a *Diamente poem* about the selected topic using words from the chart on the board.

7. Assign students to choose another topic and write a *Diamente Poem* on their own.

8. Have volunteers share their poems with the class.

Extension:

Have students write a diamente about an upcoming holiday, then use the poem as the message in a greeting card.

Notes For The Teacher:

Students may have difficulty selecting their own topic to write on. You may wish to assign a specific topic to the whole class or brainstorm possible topics and suggest that students use one of the topics from the brainstorming session.

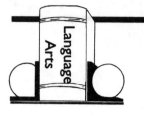

My Awful, Terrible, Horrible, No Good, Very Bad Day

Subject: Language Arts

Grade: 4-8

Time: 30+ minutes

Materials Needed:

pencils, paper, a copy of the book *Alexander and the Terrible Horrible No Good Very Bad Day* by Judith Viorst. Available for check-out at most libraries or for purchase at most bookstores.

Advance Preparation:

Objective:

Students will identify and express their experiences and feelings in writing.

Procedure:

1. Read the book *Alexander and the Terrible Horrible No Good Very Bad Day*. If the book is not available you may tell about a time when you had a bad day.

2. Have students discuss things that have happened and caused them to have a bad day. Try to discourage the discussion of morbid or disturbing events.

3. Ask students to name feelings that they have when things go wrong (you may want to list these on the board).

4. Have students write about their own *Awful, Terrible, No Good, Very Bad Day*. Remind them to include feelings in their narration.

5. Ask volunteers to share their writing with the class.

6. Collect stories for the teacher to review.

Extension:

If there is time, have the students illustrate their writing. With student permission, place the illustrated experiences in a three ring binder for students to read at their leisure.

Notes For The Teacher:

Giving students specific writing guidelines will help insure quality work. For example you may require that younger students write at least six sentences and that older students write at least three paragraphs. Providing an example you have written about a very bad day of your own will also help to get them started on the right track.

Most students enjoy listening to a good story, so classroom management should not be much of a problem while you are reading. However, it is always a good idea to explain exactly the kind of behavior you expect during an activity before you begin (feet on the floor, pencils down, eyes on the teacher, facing forward, etc.).

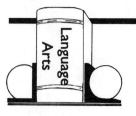

Silly Stories

Subject: Language Arts

Grade: 4-8

Time: 15 minutes

Materials Needed:

Silly Story worksheets and pencils

Advance Preparation:

Copy student worksheets.

Objective:

Students will practice naming nouns, verbs, adjectives, adverbs, and other words as they work cooperatively to compose *Silly Stories.*

Procedure:

1. Review with students the following parts of speech:

    1. Noun   = name of a person, place, or thing

    2. Verb   = shows action

    3. Adjective = describes a noun (color, size, etc.)

    4. Adverb   = describes a verb (often ends in <u>ly</u>)

2. Explain that students are going to practice naming examples of these parts of speech as they work with a partner to complete a *Silly Story.*

3. Complete the example *Silly Story* as a class.

4. Read the completed example aloud to the class.

5. Divide the class into partners and distribute the *Silly Story* worksheets.

6. Have one student provide the words for one story with the other acting as scribe and narrator. Then switch roles to complete the second *Silly Story*.

7. If time allows, students may volunteer to read their *Silly Stories* to the class.

Extension:

Trade partners and reuse the same worksheets to create new stories with a different person's input. Students in older grades may also enjoy writing their own *Silly Story* worksheets for classmates to complete.

Notes For The Teacher:

Detailed instructions and a reminder of classroom rules and expectations will help insure good classroom management during this fun activity.

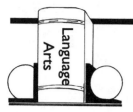
Directions: Ask a student for the part of speech or type of word as indicated. Write the word on the space provided. Repeat the process until all the spaces are filled. Read the completed *Silly Story* aloud to the class.

TRIP INTO OUTER SPACE

Last night I had a dream about you. At the age of (1) _____ you were good looking and the captain of the spaceship (2) _____. In the dream you and a crew of (3) _____ traveled to the planet (4) _____. The flight began at (5) _____ a.m. "10... 9... 8... 7... 6... 5... 4... 3... 2... 1...(6)_____ ," the controller called as the space ship blasted off from (7) _____. During take off the ship started to (8) _____ but quick action from the crew kept it on course and prevented you from crashing into (9) _____. Outer space was (10) _____ as you (11) _____ past the moon everyone (12) _____ to the windows to take a look. Finally the planet (13) _____ was in sight. After orbiting the planet (14) _____ times, while you were looking for your (15) _____ , the space ship finally landed. Everyone got off and began collecting (16) _____ (17) _____ that were all over the surface of the planet, until you started hearing (18) _____ noises. You were afraid the planet was going to explode so you hurried back on board the ship and took off (19) _____. The last thing I remember is your spaceship heading straight for the (20)_____ in my house. Boy was I ever (21) _____ to wake up!

1. number
2. proper name
3. animal (plural)
4. planet
5. time of day
6. exclamation
7. geographical location
8. verb
9. geographical location
10. adjective
11. verb (past tense)
12. verb (past tense)
13. same planet as #4
14. number
15. personal belonging
16. adjective
17. noun (plural)
18. verb ending in "ing"
19. adverb ending in "ly"
20. room in a house
21. feeling

Silly Story

MY BIRTHDAY

Yesterday was my birthday. I turned (1)_____ years old. (2) _____

took me to (3) _____ to celebrate. We (4) _____ there in an old

(5) _____ . After we arrived we went to a (6) _____ restaurant to

eat and talk about (7) _____. After everyone finished (8) _____ and

singing (9) _____ I (10)_____ out the candles and cut the

(11) _____ shaped cake. Then it was time to open my presents.

(12) _____ I exclaimed as I opened a (13) _____ wrapped box and

pulled out a (14) _____ . It's just what I always wanted for (15) _____

and never got. All in all I'd have to say it was a (16) _____ birthday.

1. number
2. person
3. geographical location
4. verb ending in "ed"
5. thing
6. adjective
7. plural noun
8. verb ending in "ing"
9. name of a song
10. verb
11. noun
12. exclamation
13. adverb ending in "ly"
14. noun
15. holiday
16. adjective

© Substitute Teaching Institute/Utah State University

Silly Story I

(to be completed by first person)

FAMILY VACATION

Last (1) _____ my family went on vacation. There were (2) _____ of us all together. We all traveled in a (3) _____ (4)_____ . It was so crowded that my pet (5) _____ whose name is (6)_____ had to ride in the (7) _____ . The trip went (8) _____ until we got lost and ended up in (9) _____ instead of (10)_____ . It was still a lot of fun. We got to see a (11) _____ (12)_____ and (13)_____ (14)_____ . My favorite part of the trip was playing (15)_____ and eating (16)_____ at (17) _____ in the morning with Aunt (18) _____ and Uncle (19)_____ . The whole trip took (20) _____ days and after hauling around all (21) _____ of my suitcases for that long I was glad to come home.

1.	month	11.	color
2.	number	12.	animal
3.	adjective	13.	adjective
4.	kind of car	14.	things
5.	animal	15.	game
6.	proper name	16.	food
7.	place in a car	17.	time
8.	adverb ending in "ly"	18.	woman's name
9.	geographical location	19.	man's name
10.	geographical location	20.	number
		21.	number

Writing for an Audience

Subject: Language Arts

Grade: 4-8

Time: 15-30 minutes

Materials Needed:

pencil, paper, and a classroom object

Advance Preparation:

Make a list of potential audiences and purposes for writing to that audience on the chalkboard.

Objective:

Students will practice writing for different audiences.

Procedure:

1. Hold up a common object in the classroom (ruler, tape dispenser, key, tablet, etc.)

2. Discuss what the object is and what it is used for.

3. Ask the students to choose an audience and purpose for writing from the board then briefly write to that audience.

4. Instruct students to not tell anyone the audience they have selected.

5. Have volunteers read their paragraphs aloud and have the class members guess which audience they selected.

Samples of Audiences and Purposes:

1. Tell a story about the object to a kindergarten class.

2. Write in a journal as though you were an archeologist who dug up this object two hundred years from now.

3. You are from another planet and you are writing home to explain how the object is used on earth.

4. Write a memo to the principal explaining why this object should be purchased for every student in the school.

5. Explain to someone who has never seen this object how it is used.

6. Write specific details about this object so that the reader could walk into the classroom and pick it out from other similar objects.

Extension:

Have students select another object in the classroom and write about it without mentioning it by name. Trade papers among class members and have them try to figure out what object the person is writing about.

Notes For The Teacher:

Setting specific guidelines for the writing assignment will help with this activity. Specify that it should be at least five sentences or that ten minutes will be all the time available for writing. The younger the students the more specific instructions they will need.

Establishing guessing procedures for step five will help with classroom management. Students will want to call out their guesses as the volunteers read their paragraphs. Establish that no one is to guess until the reader has read their entire paper and that the reader will call on someone who is raising their hand when they have finished.

Reading With Bookmarks

Subject: Language Arts

Grade: K-8

Time: Variable (time will vary with the bookmarks you select)

Materials Needed:

Select a literature book appropriate to the grade and interest level of the students. See page 254 for a list of recommended children's books.

A selection of bookmarks appropriate for the chosen book (see pages 193-194).

Materials needed to complete bookmarks (paper, crayons or markers, etc. as required).

Advance Preparation:

Select bookmarks appropriate for the chosen book and duplicate. Bookmarks can be made permanent by gluing them to construction paper or copying them onto cardstock and laminating.

Objective:

Students listen to or read a story and then respond to it via a chosen bookmark.

Procedure:

1. Read the selected book to students.

2. Show the bookmarks to the class and allow students to choose one they would like to complete.

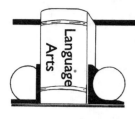
3. Allow students to work individually or in small groups to complete the projects.

4. Stress appropriate behavior if students work together in groups. Rules should include using quiet voices (six inch voices) and staying with the group.

5. Tell students the time limit.

6. Encourage students to complete more than one bookmark if time permits.

7. Display student work and/or allow students to explain their completed work.

About Bookmarks

Bookmarks can include fun activities which encourage student creativity and involvement with the characters and ideas in picture books, basal readers, or any other forms of literature. A "bookmark" is a prompt which directs students to respond to what they have been reading in a unique and creative way. On the following two pages are bookmarks adapted from the book, *Read It With Bookmarks*, by Dr. Barbara L. Goldenhersh.

In order to most effectively use these bookmarks, they should be photocopied and cut apart for distribution to individual students. Durable bookmarks can be made by mounting bookmarks on construction paper or card-stock and having them laminated. Providing each student with their own bookmark is highly recommended. If time or resources make photocopying impossible, bookmarks can be illustrated on the board. Providing several bookmark options and allowing students to choose the bookmark they want to use will encourage interest in the activity and enable students to illustrate their individual strengths.

Bookmarks can be used with reading material found in the classroom or assigned by the permanent teacher, as well as picture books you bring in your **Super SubPack**. Be sure to have available the materials (paper, pencils, crayons, markers, etc.) students will need to complete the activity and collect your bookmarks at the end of the activity for future use.

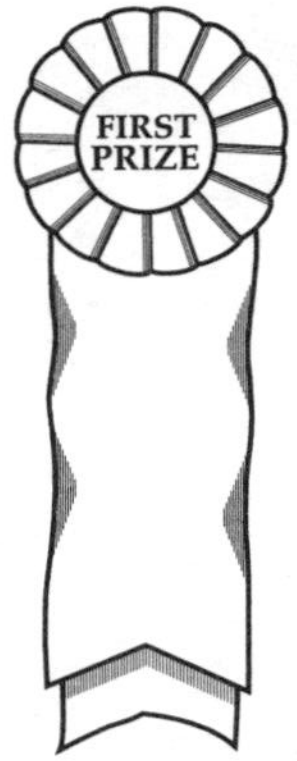

Make awards
for characters
in your book
and explain
why they
deserve them.

© Goldenhersh

Make a time line for your story.

© Goldenhersh

Predict what a
character will
be like five
years after the
book ends.

© Goldenhersh

Bookmarks adapted from "Read It With Bookmarks" by Dr. Barbara Goldenhersh.

You have ten dollars to buy a present for a character in the story. What will you buy? Why?

© Goldenhersh

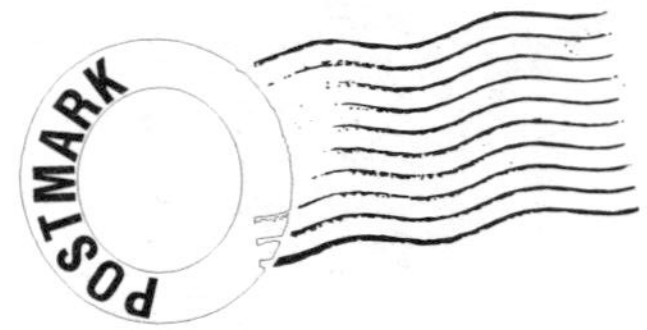

Write a letter to a friend describing the story.

POSTMARK

© Goldenhersh

If you bought this book as a gift, who would you give it to? Why?

© Goldenhersh

Bookmarks adapted from "Read It With Bookmarks" by Dr. Barbara Goldenhersh.

Tangram Stories

Subject: Language Arts

Grade: K-2 **Activity One:** *Where the Wild Things Are* by Maurice Sendak

3-8 **Activity Two:** *Grandfather Tang's Story* by Ann Tompert

Time: 30 + minutes

Materials Needed:

A set of tangrams for each student (see page 146) and the book you are planning to use in the activity.

For Activity Two, you will need to make overheads of the animal characters in the book by enlarging the diagrams in the story.

Advance Preparation:

None

Objective:

Students will use tangram pieces to create story characters.

Activity One: Where the Wild Things Are (K-2)

Procedure:

1. Give each student a set of tangrams. Give different color sets to students near one another so they will not get them mixed up when putting the tangrams away.

2. Without showing the pictures, read *Where the Wild Things Are* to the point where Max is sent to bed without any supper.

© Substitute Teaching Institute/Utah State University

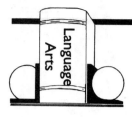

3. Have students each make Max using their tangrams.

4. Ask students how many made their Max using one, two, three, etc. pieces. Compare the various Max creations. Talk about the shapes used to create the individual pictures.

5. Read on in the story until reaching the boat.

6. Have students make the boat and discuss as above.

7. Continue the story until the Monsters have their "rumpus."

8. Allow students to create monsters and discuss as above.

9. Complete the book.

10. Ask students to place the seven tangram pieces back in the bag and return it to you.

Extension:

Allow students to create their own book of *Where the Wild Things Are* using paper tangram sets to make the illustrations.

Activity Two: Grandfather Tang's Story (3-8)

Procedure:

1. Pair the students up. (By pairing students with someone sitting next to them, you are less likely to pair problem students together as the teacher has likely separated such students.)

2. Give each student a set of tangrams. Give different color sets to student pairs so they do not get the sets confused. Assign students on the right to take the part of *Chou* and those on the left to be *Wu Ling*.

3. Begin reading *Grandfather Tang's Story* to the point where Grandfather creates the two foxes.

4. Display tangram character overhead and have students make their assigned character using their tangrams.

5. Continue reading until the characters change themselves into other animals. Allow students to make their animal.

6. Continue reading and stopping to allow students to make each animal their character turns into.

7. Continue until the end of the story.

8. Explain the history of tangrams as explained at the end of the book.

9. Ask students to place the seven tangram pieces back in the bag and return them to you.

Extensions:

Language Arts: Allow students to write their own fox fairy story using characters they create.

Math: Have students determine whether they can make a square using one piece, two pieces, three pieces, four pieces, five pieces, six pieces, and seven pieces.

Notes For The Teacher:

You may want to leave a tangram pattern for the teacher as students tend to be intrigued by these activities and want to have their own tangram set.

Other
Language Arts Activities

Literature in the Classroom

Literature can enhance learning at every grade level. When sharing literature books, use creative questioning to keep students interested. A question which requires a single right answer does little to keep students involved. Questions which have a variety of answers will keep students engaged in discussion and move learning forward. Ask students what they would do in a similar situation, what else the character might have done, what would be different if the setting or era were changed in the story, etc. Ask them to justify actions and evaluate occurrences. Have trials of story predators or write letters to the author. If you can get students involved in the story, positive behavior will be a natural result. For a list of recommended children's literature see page 254.

The Newspaper

The newspaper can be a lifesaver when substitute teaching. If there were no plans left for a classroom, the newspaper can be used to teach anything! In a kindergarten class, students can circle letters of the alphabet and even do a dot to dot with those letters. In first grade, students could circle words they recognize or discuss the emotions depicted in pictures. At various grade levels, students could create a shopping list from ads, forecast weather and discuss climate, work out statistics for sporting events, write want ads or cartoons, or create a budget using data from job opportunities, apartment rental, and food advertisement sections. Just use some creativity and you can teach anything!

Prompts

The following prompts have been adapted from *The Kids' Book of Questions* by Gregory Stock, Ph.D. These prompts can be used for writing activities or for class discussions. There are no right or wrong answers, only an opportunity for students to explore their own thoughts, values, and beliefs. Encourage students to explain and justify their responses. Do not allow students to criticize the thoughts and opinions of others.

Prompts for Student Response

1. If this weekend you could do anything you wanted to, what would you do?

2. If you were a teacher and the students in your class wouldn't stop talking what would you do? What if you did that and they still didn't stop talking?

3. If you could live someone else's life for three days, who would you choose and why?

4. If you knew it would save the lives of 10 children by not buying any new clothes for the next year would you do it?

5. If there was a poster contest coming up, would you rather create a poster all by yourself and get all of the credit, or work with a group and share the credit with the other group members.

6. Would it be worse to spend a night all alone in an empty house without electricity or with a friend camping in the forest during a thunderstorm?

7. If you had agreed to sell your roller blades to a friend and then someone else offered you more money, what would you do?

8. If you could be invisible for one day, what would you do?

9. If your parents were going to be living in a foreign country for the next year, would you rather go with them or stay in your own neighborhood with a friend?

10. What would the perfect day at school be like?

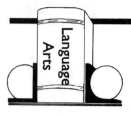

11. If your favorite pet needed an expensive operation and the only way your family could afford it was not to give birthday presents for the next two years, would you want your pet to have the operation?

12. If you could change just one thing about school, what would you change?

13. Pretend you could only have one pair of shoes for the next year. Would you choose shoes which are really comfortable but look a kind of goofy, or shoes that look really cool but are uncomfortable to wear?

14. What are two things you don't like now, but ten years from now you don't think will be so bad?

15. If you had to pick a new first and last name for yourself, what would be your top three choices?

16. Suppose your dad forgot that he had promised to drive you and a friend to the movies one Saturday afternoon; he went golfing instead. If you could choose a punishment for your dad, what would it be? Do you think it would make him not do this again?

17. What subjects in school do you think are really important to study? Why?

18. Would you rather be a rich and famous movie star, or an unkown scientist who discovers a cure for cancer? Why?

19. If you could pick any age, and be that age for the rest of your life, what age would you want to be? Why?

20. If you could choose new jobs for your parents, what would you choose and why?

How Many Are There?

Subject: Math

Grade: K-5

Time: 15-30 minutes

Materials:

chalkboard and chalk

Advance Preparation:

Objective:

Students will categorize and count their classmates in various ways.

Procedure:

1. Discuss ways that class members are alike, and different, (eye color, month they were born, number of letters in their name, etc.)

2. Make a grid on the board similar to the one below using one of the categories mentioned above.

When We Were Born

Jan	Feb	Mar	Apr	May	June	July	Aug	Sept	Oct	Nov	Dec

3. Complete the grid as a class.

4. Have the students determine which column has the most and which has the least.

5. Summarize by explaining that all things can be categorized in different ways.

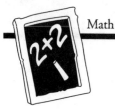

6. Have the students decide another way to categorize the class and complete a second grid.

Extension:

Discuss situations where the information from the grids may be useful.

Extension:

Assign students to independently make a grid categorizing the members of their family in some way.

Notes For The Teacher:

Developing an organized method for determining and recording grid information will help significantly with classroom management during this activity. For example, fill in the columns one by one by having students who should be counted for each column raise their hand as you come to it. Ask another student, who is not being counted, to count the hands raised and enter the number on the grid.

Shapes

Name _____

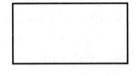

Directions For The Teacher: Read the instructions aloud to the class allowing time for students to complete each activity before going on the next one. If students are able to read you may wish to complete number one as a class then assign students to complete the rest of the page individually or in small groups.

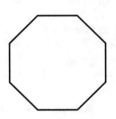

1. A circle has no straight sides
    Color the circle red.

2. A triangle has 3 straight sides.
    Color the triangle blue.

3. A square has 4 sides that are all the same length.
    Color the square yellow.

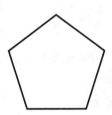

4. A rectangle has 4 sides but they are not all the same length.
    Color the rectangle brown.

5. A pentagon has 5 sides.
    Color the pentagon orange.

6. A hexagon has 6 sides.
    Color the hexagon purple.

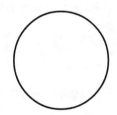

7. A heptagon has 7 sides.
    Color the heptagon pink.

8. An octagon has 8 sides.
    Color the octagon green.

9. A nonagon has 9 sides.
    Color the nonagon black.

10. A decagon has 10 sides.
    Draw a happy face inside the decagon.

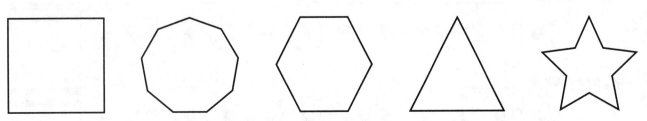

Calculator Flights

Name _____

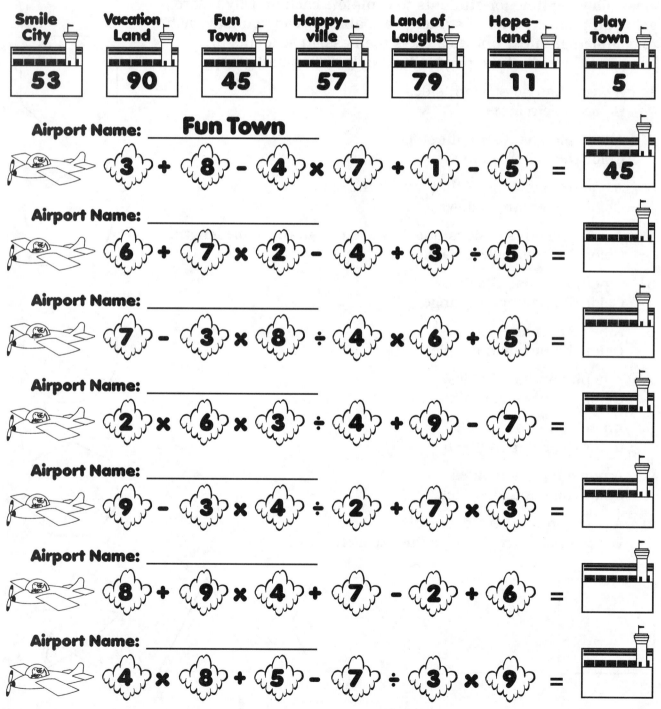

Grades
2-6

Use a calculator to solve each problem. Write the answer in the airport at the end of the problem. Find the airport that matches the answer and write its name above the plane. Remember to press "C" (clear) before going on to the next problem. An example has been done for you.

Smile City	Vacation Land	Fun Town	Happy-ville	Land of Laughs	Hope-land	Play Town
53	90	45	57	79	11	5

Airport Name: **Fun Town**

3 + 8 − 4 × 7 + 1 − 5 = 45

Airport Name: _____

6 + 7 × 2 − 4 + 3 ÷ 5 =

Airport Name: _____

7 − 3 × 8 ÷ 4 × 6 + 5 =

Airport Name: _____

2 × 6 × 3 ÷ 4 + 9 − 7 =

Airport Name: _____

9 − 3 × 4 ÷ 2 + 7 × 3 =

Airport Name: _____

8 + 9 × 4 + 7 − 2 + 6 =

Airport Name: _____

4 × 8 + 5 − 7 ÷ 3 × 9 =

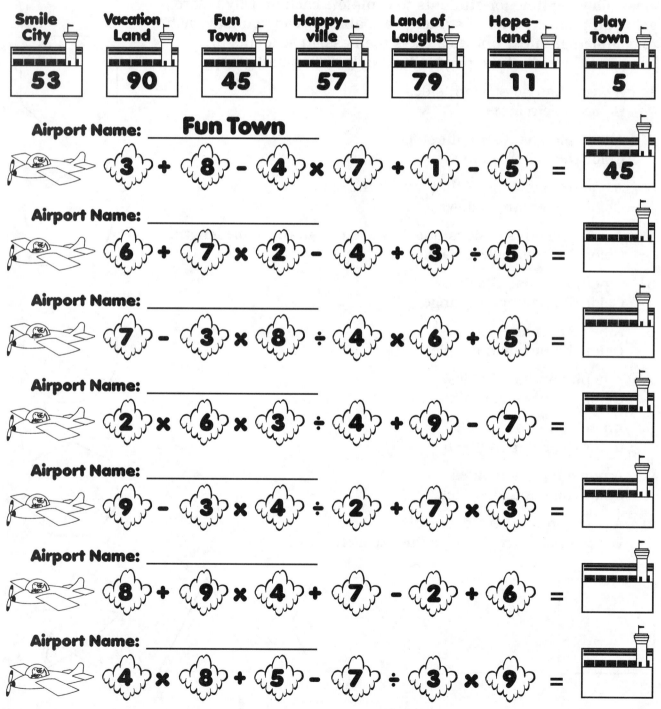

Substitute Teaching Institute/Utah State University

Number Search

Subject: Math

Grade: 3-6

Time: 30 minutes

Materials Needed:

pencil and *Number Search* worksheet

Advance Preparation:

Make a copy of the *Number Search* worksheet for each student in the class.

Objective:

Students will practice single digit addition and subtraction facts in a fun and challenging way.

Procedure:

1. Distribute worksheets.

2. Explain that a number search is like a word search except students will be searching for number equations instead of words.

3. Review directions on the worksheets.

4. Illustrate how to find and circle an equation.

5. Have students complete the work sheet and hand it in for teacher evaluation.

Extension:

Using copies of the *Number Puzzle Grid*, found at the end of this lesson, have students create their own number search puzzles then exchange and complete among class members.

Math

Notes For The Teacher:

Some Students become easily frustrated with this type of activity when they can't find all of the answers. One way to alleviate some of their frustration and promote cooperative learning is to allow students to work toegther in groups to find the solutions. Another way is to have students work independently at the beginning of the activity then allow group work for the last five to seven minutes. This will help to insure that everyone completes the activity and has a successful experience.

9	0	2	1	4	7	8	3	2	2	4	8	9	1	1
4	2	9	7	8	0	2	4	5	8	3+	3=	6	8	9
0	0	2+	6=	8	9	4	2	1	2	2	4	3	2	1
1	8	0	9	5	4	7	5	9	2	7	6	9	0	9
5	6+	4	3+	2=	5	7	9	0	8	2	4	2	1	1
0	9	1	2	4	8	5	7	0	8	6	9	0	7	9

Directions: Solve, find, and circle each number equation in the puzzle.

Equations to find:

1.   3 + 2 =

2.   6 + 0 =

3.   5 + 4 =

4.   3 + 3 =

5.   8 - 2 =

6.   2 + 6 =

Number Search

Name _____

8	6	2	6	9	2	4	3	6	7	8	1	3	4	0
1	3	6	9	7	0	3	6	8	0	0	3	5	2	1
3	2	4	8	9	0	1	7	5	9	2	1	8	9	2
3	7	6	9	2	7	8	7	3	6	7	2	9	2	8
0	9	7	4	8	2	7	1	9	6	7	8	5	6	0
2	9	0	1	2	7	8	9	0	1	3	4	6	9	2
1	7	9	5	6	4	7	6	9	9	3	5	6	2	0
2	5	3	5	6	7	4	2	4	0	2	9	8	0	3
5	2	7	1	9	3	0	8	9	6	3	5	6	8	2
3	8	9	2	8	5	8	2	0	4	7	5	9	6	1
3	8	0	2	4	8	9	0	1	8	9	4	6	8	2
7	4	2	3	2	4	3	0	9	8	8	6	9	0	4
8	9	3	2	4	5	8	6	1	6	3	6	8	9	0

Directions: Solve, find, and circle the number equations:

Example: 8 + 1 = **9**

1. ____ 5 + 2 = ____
2. ____ 6 + 2 = ____
3. ____ 9 - 9 = ____
4. ____ 2 + 2 + 5 = ____
5. ____ 1 + 2 = ____

6. ____ 3 + 5 = ____
7. ____ 2 + 7 = ____
8. ____ 4 + 4 = ____
9. ____ 8 - 6 = ____
10. ____ 4 + 3 + 1 = ____

11. ____ 4 + 2 + 3 = ____
12. ____ 9 - 8 = ____
13. ____ 4 - 3 = ____
14. ____ 2 + 1 + 2 = ____
15. ____ 9 - 6 = ____

Number Search

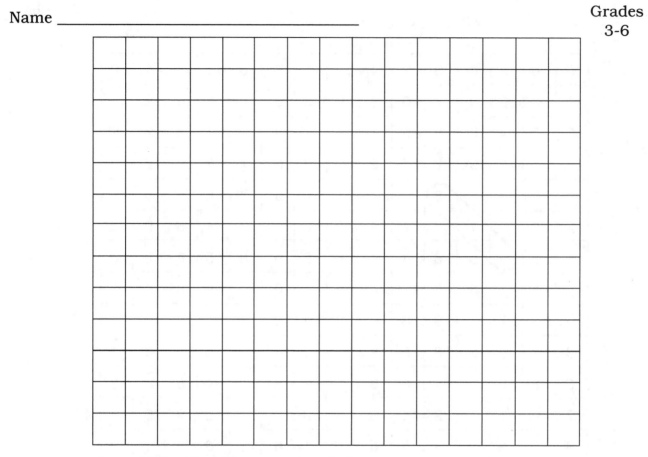

1.   Write 15 number equations below.
2.   Put the numbers for the equations in the chart above.
3.   Fill in the rest of the chart with other numbers.
4.   Trade papers with someone in the class.

1. _____   6. _____   11. _____

2. _____   7. _____   12. _____

3. _____   8. _____   13. _____

4. _____   9. _____   14. _____

5. _____   10. _____   15. _____

Graph Art

Subject: Math

Grade: 3-8

Time: 15-30 minutes

Materials Needed:

Graph Art worksheets, pencils, and crayons

Advance Preparation:

Copy worksheets and determine six points to be used in the art activity.

Objective:

Students will learn to plot points on a graph and create an image which incorporates several plotted points.

Procedures:

1. Teach or review with students how to plot a point on a graph (see *Notes For The Teacher*).

2. Distribute graph worksheets and have students plot six pre-determined points.

3. Make sure the points are dark enough to be seen on the back side of the paper.

4. Demonstrate or show examples of graph art (see next page).

5. Explain the rules for Graph Art.

    1. All dots must be connected.

    2. A dot may connect more than once.

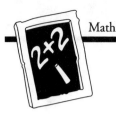

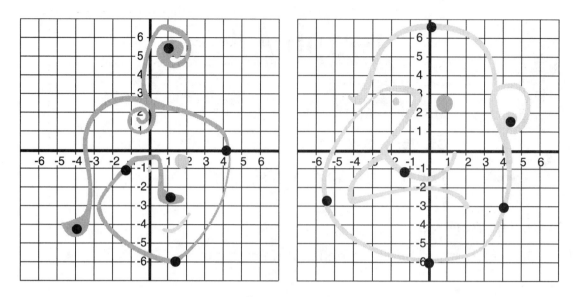

Graph Art Examples

3. All dots must be used.

4. Other lines may be added to create the picture.

6. Have the students turn their paper over and use the dots to create their own graph art.

7. if time allows, color the artwork.

8. Turn in artwork for classroom display. It is fun to see different pictures that all contain the same six dots.

Extension:

Number and display pictures without the students' names visible. Have each class member vote by secret ballot for their three favorite works of art. Tally the votes on the board and award a prize to the classroom winner.

Notes For The Teacher:

Making copies of or keeping graph art done by previous classes is a great way to collect a portfolio of examples. Often students who finish early are more than willing to make another picture for you to keep and show to other classes.

Background Information On Plotting Points

A point on a graph can be found using a pair of numbers. The number pair for a point is called its coordinates. The *first* number in the pair tells how far to go right or left. The *second* number in the pair tells how far to go up or down. Below are examples of how to find points from coordinates.

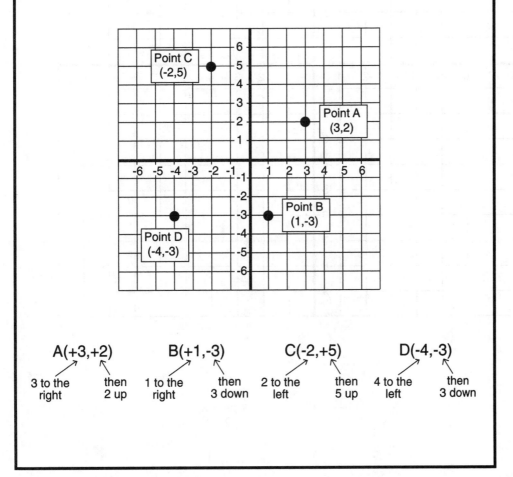

Graph Art

Name _____

Survey And Graph

Subject: Math

Grade: 4-8

Time: 30+ minutes

Materials Needed:

pencil and paper

Advance Preparation:

Objective:

Students will survey the class on a topic of interest, create a bar graph to illustrate the results, and develop questions relating to the information collected.

Procedure:

1. Conduct a class survey on a topic of interest. (favorite candy bar, color, professional football team, etc.)

2. Have the students construct a bar graph illustrating the results of the survey. (see example on next page)

3. Have students write three questions that require using the bar graph to determine the correct answer. (see example below)

4. Exchange papers among classmates and have them answer each other's questions.

5. Be sure that both the student who wrote the questions and the student who answered them are clearly identified on the paper, then hand in for teacher evaluation.

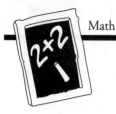

Example Bar Graph and Questions

Favorite Cookie Graph

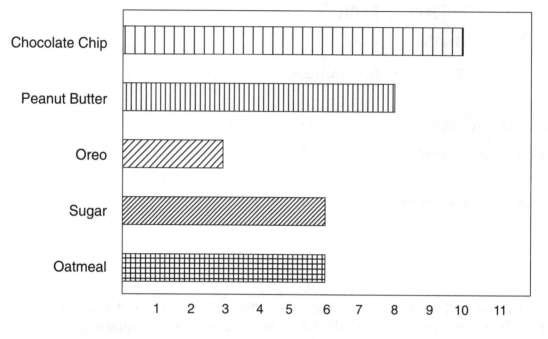

Questions:

1. How many more students voted for Oatmeal than Oreo Cookies? _____

2. What were the total number of votes for Peanut Butter and Sugar cookies combined? _____

3. Which kind of cookie got the most votes? _____

Extension:

Have students develop individual surveys to conduct outside of class. Assign them to survey 30 people, at lunch, during recess, etc. After the surveys are complete assign students to construct bar graphs to be compiled in a book or displayed in the classroom for other students to see.

Notes For The Teacher:

Finding an organized way to conduct the class survey will help with classroom management during this activity. One method is to have students write their answers on a piece of paper. Collect the papers and have one student read the results while another tallies the information on the board. The students love to participate like this and it leaves the teacher free to monitor the class and deal with any disruptive behavior without interrupting the progress of the lesson.

It is also helpful in classrooms where students have not had much graph experience to model the bar graph on the board while they construct their own on paper.

Calendar Math

JANUARY
S	M	T	W	Th	F	S
						1
2	3	4	5	6	7	8
9	10	11	12	13	14	15
16	17	18	19	20	21	22
23	24	25	26	27	28	29
30	31					

FEBRUARY
S	M	T	W	Th	F	S
		1	2	3	4	5
6	7	8	9	10	11	12
13	14	15	16	17	18	19
20	21	22	23	24	25	26
27	28	29				

MARCH
S	M	T	W	Th	F	S
			1	2	3	4
5	6	7	8	9	10	11
12	13	14	15	16	17	18
19	20	21	22	23	24	25
26	27	28	29	30	31	

APRIL
S	M	T	W	Th	F	S
						1
2	3	4	5	6	7	8
9	10	11	12	13	14	15
16	17	18	19	20	21	22
23	24	25	26	27	28	29
30						

MAY
S	M	T	W	Th	F	S
	1	2	3	4	5	6
7	8	9	10	11	12	13
14	15	16	17	18	19	20
21	22	23	24	25	26	27
28	29	30	31			

JUNE
S	M	T	W	Th	F	S
				1	2	3
4	5	6	7	8	9	10
11	12	13	14	15	16	17
18	19	20	21	22	23	24
25	26	27	28	29	30	

JULY
S	M	T	W	Th	F	S
						1
2	3	4	5	6	7	8
9	10	11	12	13	14	15
16	17	18	19	20	21	22
23	24	25	26	27	28	29
30	31					

AUGUST
S	M	T	W	Th	F	S
		1	2	3	4	5
6	7	8	9	10	11	12
13	14	15	16	17	18	19
20	21	22	23	24	25	26
27	28	29	30	31		

SEPTEMBER
S	M	T	W	Th	F	S
					1	2
3	4	5	6	7	8	9
10	11	12	13	14	15	16
17	18	19	20	21	22	23
24	25	26	27	28	29	30

OCTOBER
S	M	T	W	Th	F	S
1	2	3	4	5	6	7
8	9	10	11	12	13	14
15	16	17	18	19	20	21
22	23	24	25	26	27	28
29	30	31				

NOVEMBER
S	M	T	W	Th	F	S
			1	2	3	4
5	6	7	8	9	10	11
12	13	14	15	16	17	18
19	20	21	22	23	24	25
26	27	28	29	30		

DECEMBER
S	M	T	W	Th	F	S
					1	2
3	4	5	6	7	8	9
10	11	12	13	14	15	16
17	18	19	20	21	22	23
24	25	26	27	28	29	30
31						

1. How many days are there between March 5th and October 30th? _____

2. How many months have names with four or less letters in their name? _____

3. How many days are in these "short name" months combined? _____

4. How many days are there in the month you were born? _____

5. Laws require that there are 180 days in a school year. If school started on August 15 and you went seven days a week without any days off for holidays or weekends, when would summer vacation begin? _____

6. Suppose there was a law that allowed you to attend school only on odd numbered dates, Monday through Friday. How many days would you attend school in the month of October? _____

7. There are 24 hours in one day. How many hours are there in the month of June? _____

8. There are 365 days in a year (excluding leap year). Figure out, as of today, how many days old you are. _____

9. Which months have 30 days?   Which have 31 days?

_____ _____ | _____ _____

_____ _____ | _____ _____

_____ _____ | _____ _____

_____ _____ | _____ _____

10. Which month did you not list in the previous question? _____

11. If you left on April 26th for a 14 day vacation to Hawaii, on what day would you return home? _____

12. How many school days are there between February 26 and April 19? _____

13. What is something you remember from last year? _____

14. If school lets out for summer vacation on June 1 and begins again on August 28, how many days of summer vacation do you get? _____

15. How many Mondays are there in the month of October? _____

16. How many days are there between Christmas Day and New Years Day? _____

17. Do any months in the calendar have a Friday the 13th? _____ Which one(s)?

_____

18. How many days are there between Valentine's Day and Independence Day? _____

19. Suppose you only went to school on Monday, Wednesday, and Friday. How many days would you go to school in the month of March? _____

20. Think up your own Calendar Math Question and have someone else answer it.

Question: _____

_____

Answer: _____

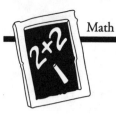

Calendar Math ANSWER KEY

1. 238 days

2. 3 months

3. 92 days

4. answers will vary

5. February 10

6. 11 days

7. 720 hours

8. answers will vary

9. 30 Days: April, June, September, November / 31 Days: January, March, May, July, August, October, December

10. February

11. May 9

12. 37 days

13. answers will vary

14. 88 days

15. 5 Mondays

16. 6 days

17. Yes; October

18. 140 days

19. 14 days

20. answers will vary

Science Experiments, Tricks, and Activities

The activities on this page can be used in a number of different ways. With little, or no preparation they can fill an extra few minutes at the end of class or be presented as part of a lesson.

Not a Knot?

Equipment: Two or three feet of string.

Procedure: Lay the string out on a table. Hold one end in each hand, and pose the problem of how to tie a knot in it without letting go of either end.

Solution: Fold your arms, pick up each end, and unfold your arms. There will be a knot in the string because there was a "knot" in your arms.

Getting a Rise

Equipment: sheet of paper and two books

Procedure: Suspend the paper by placing the books under each end. Blow straight under the paper, and it will bend downward, not upward as expected.

Explanation: Air in motion exerts less lateral or side pressure than air at rest or moving more slowly. When air is blown under the paper, it exerts less pressure than the still air above it. The still air then pushes the paper down. This is the principle by which airplanes fly.

Look for additional science activities and experiments in books at your local library.

Feeling Sound

Subject: Science

Grade: K-5

Time: 15 minutes

Materials Needed:

tuning fork, small dish of water, soft rubber mallet or rubber heel from a shoe

Advance Preparation:

Objective:

Students will feel and observe the effects of sound waves created by a tuning fork.

Procedure:

1. Hold the tuning fork in one hand and strike it with the rubber mallet or shoe heel.

2. Explain that sound is made by producing vibrations. As the end of the tuning fork vibrates, sound is produced.

3. Have students remain seated while the teacher walks around to each desk striking the tuning fork and allowing the student to move their hand close to the double end, feel the vibrations, and eventually touch the double end thereby stopping the sound.

4. Ask students why the sound stopped when they touched the double end of the tuning fork. (Because they stopped the vibrations.)

5. Tell the students that you are going to strike the tuning fork and then place the double end in a small dish of water. Ask them to predict what will happen.

6. When the tines of the fork are lowered slowly into the water, the water will splash demonstrating that vibration is occurring.

7. Have the students list five or more things they learned about sound from this lesson on the board.

Extension:

Demonstrate that placing the handle of the tuning fork to a desk or other hard surface after it has been struck will make the sound louder. Have students think of other ideas to make the sound louder, then test their ideas.

Notes For The Teacher:

Tuning forks may be obtained from many sources including music stores, science supply houses, and medical supply stores. Children who play stringed musical instruments may have them for tuning their instruments. Specially designed tuning forks are used by doctors for hearing tests.

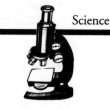

Touchy Feely Scavenger Hunt

Subject: Science

Grade: K-5

Time: 15-30 minutes

Materials Needed:

paper and pencil

Advance Preparation:

Objective:

Students will become more aware of the different textures that make up various objects.

Procedure:

1. Have students identify the five senses (sight, touch, taste, smell, and hearing).

2. Discuss the sense of touch and how it is used.

3. Brainstorm 15-20 words that describe how things feel (soft, fuzzy, hard, cold, rough, etc.)

4. Have students, either individually or in groups, list these words on their papers. Then conduct a scavenger hunt around the classroom listing objects that *"feel"* like the word when they *"touch"* it.

5. Discuss the following as a class:

    1. What was the most difficult *"feel"* to find?

    2. What textures do you like best?

    3. Why are different textures used for different things?

Extension:

Conduct a second scavenger hunt outside the classroom such as on the playground. Compare the differences in textures found outside, with those found inside.

Extension:

Have students write a creative story about what the world would be like if everything "felt" the same.

Notes For The Teacher:

Be sure to remind students of expected classroom behavior during the scavenger hunt (i.e. walking and talking quietly, keeping hands, feet, and objects to yourself).

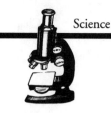

Balloon Reactions

Subject: Science

Grade: 2-8

Time: 15 minutes

Materials Needed:

two balloons of the same size, two pieces of string 60 cm (2 ft.) long, wool cloth

Advance Preparation:

Procedure:

1. Inflate balloons and tie the ends with string.

2. Hold the balloons so that they hang about one to two inches apart.

3. Rub one of the balloons with the wool cloth and repeat step two.

4. Observe what happens. (The balloons attract then repel each other after touching.)

5. Rub the other balloon with the wool cloth and repeat step two again.

6. Observe what happens. (The balloons repel each other.)

7. Ask the students if they can explain what they observed.

8. Teach about static electricity to complete or correct student explanations as needed (see *Notes For The Teacher/ Background Information*).

Extension:

Complete the activity again substituting strips of plastic for balloons. Ask the students to predict and explain the outcome of each step.

Notes For The Teacher:

Static electricity works best on cool clear days, but success should be attainable except perhaps on an extremely hot and muggy day. As you select the wool cloth for this activity make sure it has not been treated with anti-cling products which would inhibit the production and transfer of static electricity.

Background Information:

As in many other aspects of life, when dealing with static electricity opposites attract. When the balloons in this activity are placed near one another in step two they are both neutral and so there is no reaction. The wool cloth used in step three gives up electrons to the balloon and causes it to be negatively charged. Thus in step four the balloons attract each other until they touch. Upon contact the negatively charged balloon gives up some of it's electrons and causes the other to also be negatively charged and so they begin to repel one another. When both balloons have been rubbed with the wool in step five they are both negatively charged and will repel each other.

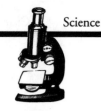

Eco-Mural

Subject: Science

Grade: 3-8

Time: 30+ minutes

Materials Needed:

four large mural size sheets of paper, eco-cards, pencils, and crayons or markers

Advance Preparation:

Copy and cut apart the eco-cards.

Objective:

Students will learn about the components of different ecosystems as they exist in various environments.

Procedure:

1. Discuss that an ecosystem is a group of things, both living and nonliving, which exist together in an area and help one another to survive.

2. Explain that students are going to work in groups to draw a mural of an ecosystem by depicting the parts of the ecosystem listed on a set of cards given to each group.

3. Explain the rules for the activity.

    A. Everyone must participate.
    B. All cards must be represented in the mural.
    C. Other things that could be found in the ecosystem may be added to the picture.
    D. The name of the ecosystem must be printed on the mural.
    E. The names of those who created the mural should also appear on the picture.

4. Divide the class into four groups.

5. Assign a group captain from each group.

6. Distribute the mural paper, pencils, and art supplies to each group.

7. Give the group captain the eco-cards for each group to distribute among the group members.

8. Assign group captains the responsibility of making sure that everyone participates and that all of the eco-cards are represented in the mural.

9. Set a time limit for the completion of the murals (students will need 25-30 minutes).

10. Students complete the *Eco-Murals*.

11. Collect the eco-cards for future use.

12. Have volunteers from each group explain their ecosystem.

13. Turn in *Eco-Murals* for classroom display.

Extension:

Discuss what would happen if one or more parts of the ecosystem were destroyed. How would it affect the rest of the ecosystem?

Notes For The Teacher:

Students may have difficulty organizing and completing their murals. You may wish to suggest the following steps for groups to follow:

1. Group Captain reads the cards out loud.

2. The group decides what kind of an ecosystem they will be drawing.

3. The mural is outlined by placing the cards on the paper where the pictures will be.

4. Everyone then begins replacing the cards with pictures.

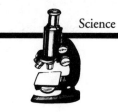

ECO-CARDS

OCEAN	DESERT	WETLAND	FOREST
sun	sun	sun	sun
water	sand	ponds	waterfall
starfish	rocks	marshy ground	fallen logs
fish	snakes	frogs	deer
sharks	camels	fish	birds
octopus	spiders	birds	chipmunks
seaweed	cactus	tall grass	pine trees
algae	sage brush	water lilies	bushes
whale	lizards	moss covered rocks	lake

Knowing Nonpoint

Subject: Science

Grade: 3-8

Time: 30 minutes

Materials Needed:

broom, recycled paper (3 sheets per student), and role cards (duplicate and cut out so each student has one)

Advance Preparation:

Photocopy and cut apart the role cards.

Objective:

This lesson will introduce the concept of nonpoint pollution.

Procedure:

Activity One

1.   Place the term nonpoint pollution on the board. Ask students what they think the term means. Accept all answers, but do not define the term. Indicate that the activity they are going to do next will demonstrate nonpoint pollution.

2.   Distribute role cards.

3.   Introduce the activity by discussing how the different groups represented on the cards can pollute water.

4.   Distribute three sheets of recycled paper to each student. Instruct them to list a different pollutant that could come from the source on their role card on each of the three papers. Then tell them to wad up each paper and throw it on the floor.

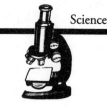

Example: If a student were given a paper that says: "You like to work on your car at home," the student might write on three separate pieces of paper:

A.   Oil from my car dumped on the ground.

B.   Spilled antifreeze.

C.   Cleaning solution and grease from my car poured down the drain.

5.   Assign a person to be the "rain person." Use a broom to sweep the paper into a pile.

6.   Place the headings Agriculture, Mining/Logging, Urban (business/home), Waste Disposal, and Construction on the chalkboard. Unfold each paper and list each pollutant under the appropriate heading.

7.   Once the list is completed on the board, discuss the results with the class. Was the oil from just one car harmful? Was the oil from all the cars harmful? Even though each student only dropped three pieces of paper, look how much it added up to.

8.   Discuss your community's water supply. Where does it come from? What might contaminate it?

Extension:

Activity Two

Create mountain ranges of aluminum foil. Sprinkle pepper and drop some red, blue, and green food coloring on different parts of the mountain range. Use a spray bottle to make it rain, and collect the runoff. What does it look like? Where did the pollution come from? What can be done to clean it up? What could have been done before it rained?

Notes for the teachers:

Some say the industry and sewage plants are the major causes of pollution in our water today. The fact is that 99 percent of sediment, 84 percent of phosphates, and 99 percent of nitrates entering the nation's lakes and streams come from other sources. These sources are called nonpoint source (NPS).

Nonpoint Role Cards

You are a farmer who grows wheat and corn.	You are a farmer who grows apples and grapes.	You are a rancher who raises sheep.
You are a farmer who raises pigs.	You drive five miles to work every day.	You are in charge of an airport.
You are a farmer who raises cattle.	You operate a large grocery store.	You operate a zoo.
You like to work on your car at home.	You own a gas station with large underground tanks.	You like to keep your house clean.
You are a principal of a large school.	You are in charge of your city streets.	You own a large logging company.
You produce coal from your mine.	You produce copper from your mine.	You are in charge of a landfill.
You have a large lawn.	You are in charge of building new roads in your town.	You are a major contractor in your community.

Silent Lesson

Subject: Adaptable

Grade: K-8

Time: Variable

Materials Needed:

Awards for students who remain silent throughout the entire lesson.

Advance Preparation:

Objective:

Students will practice written and other nonverbal communication skills.

Procedure:

1. If students are old enough to read, begin the lesson by not talking and simply start writing the silent lesson rules on the board. If students cannot read, explain the rules verbally before beginning.

    Silent Lesson Rules

    1. No Talking.

    2. If you need to ask a question, write it down.

    3. The teacher cannot talk either.

    4. Awards will be given to students who remain silent for the whole lesson.

    5. The silent lesson will begin now and continue until _____ . (establish a time)

2. Hand out a seat work activity or give instructions for another assignment by writing them on the board.

3. Monitor students' work and silence.

4. Answer any questions by writing down a response.

5. Students who finish early can communicate with each other by writing notes.

6. Award prizes to students who remained silent throughout the entire lesson.

Extension:

Discuss what students learned about communicating without being able to talk.

Notes For The Teacher:

This lesson works well to quiet students down after recess, P.E., or any other energizing activity.

This activity will be the most fun and least frustrating for both you and the students if it is used with an assignment or worksheet that requires little, if any, teacher explanation.

Another variation of this activity is to give each student three stickers or pieces of colored paper. One is taken away each time the student talks. The number of stickers the student has left at the end of the activity determines the level of the prize they receive.

Poster Contest

Subject: Adaptable

Grade: K-8

Time: 30+ minutes

Materials Needed:

pencil, paper, crayons and other art supplies

Advance Preparation:

Objective:

Students will create a poster which reflects something they have learned in a recent lesson.

Procedure:

1. Review concepts or ideas that students have studied in a lesson that day.

2. List these concepts and ideas on the board.

3. Set a time limit for having the posters completed.

4. Have students create a poster depicting some aspect of the lesson.

5. Collect posters for teacher evaluation and classroom display.

Extension:

Have volunteers explain their posters to the class.

Extension:

Display posters and have the class vote for their three favorite ones. Award winners.

Notes For The Teacher:

It is often helpful to display posters created by students in previous classes you have taught, to give students a concrete example of what they are trying to accomplish.

Adaptable

Bingo Review

Subject: Adaptable

Grade: 3-8

Time: 30+ minutes

Materials Needed:

Bingo Review worksheet, pencils, small objects to mark the bingo squares (pieces of colored paper, beans, etc.), and prizes for the winners

Advance Preparation:

Identify 25 terms that students have been studying recently. Science, spelling, or vocabulary words work well. Students can help you compile this list.

Objective:

Students will review terms or concepts they have been studying.

Procedure:

1. Establish that participating in this activity is a privilege and that anyone who behaves inappropriately (i.e. flipping their markers across the room or calling out answers), will not be allowed to participate.

2. Distribute one bingo sheet to each student.

3. List the 25 words on the board and have the students copy them randomly onto their bingo sheet.

    NOTE: Stress the importance of copying the words so that their sheet is like no one else's.

4. Distribute the bingo markers.

5. Using your own list, randomly select a term and provide the class with a clue or definition of the word.

6. Students raise their hands to guess the answer.

7. When the correct answer is determined, everyone marks that spot on their sheet.

8. Steps 5-7 are repeated until someone has bingo with 5 squares marked in a row.

9. Continue play until three people have won.

10. Award prizes to the winners.

11. If time allows, have students clear their sheets and play again.

Extension:

At the conclusion of the game have students turn their sheets over and define each word or use it correctly in a sentence.

Notes For The Teacher:

Be firm, fair, and consistent in maintaining expected student behavior during this activity. It will make it more enjoyable for you and the other students in the class.

If time is limited, alter the game so that three or four in a row constitutes bingo.

If you are teaching in a middle or junior high school, save the bingo sheets from the first class and use them again and again throughout the day.

Bingo Review

Name _____

Substitute Teaching Institute/Utah State University

Letter Challenge

Grades
3-8

Name _____

SUBJECT WORD	Food	State or Country	Sport or Game	Movie or T.V. Show	Boy's Name	Girl's Name	Adjective	Article of Clothing	Animal

Place a word in the far left column, then write words in each of the subject areas that begin with the letter in that row. Use subject words that are part of a lesson or unit being taught.

Appendix

Glossary

Abuse
The physical, sexual, or emotional maltreatment of children.

Acknowledge and Restate
Classroom management strategy that involves verbally acknowledging student protests or outbursts, then restating expected behavior. Acknowledging a student's comment, validates them as a person and will often diffuse an emotionally charged situation. Phrases such as, "I can tell that you" and "It is obvious that" can be used to acknowledging what the student said. Transition words such as "however," "but," and "nevertheless," bring the dialogue back to the expected behavior. Example: "I can tell that you are not very interested in this topic, nevertheless the assignment is to write a 500 word essay about music and you are expected to have it completed by the end of class." (see also I Understand)

Active Response
A questioning response that requires thought, evaluation, or synthesis of information on the part of the student giving the response.

Active Viewer
A student who views a video, filmstrip, or other audio visual presentation while actively engaging in thought about what they are seeing and hearing. Two forms of active engagement include note taking during the presentation and watching for specific information to answer questions after the presentation.

Anecdotal Records
Records of the date, place, time, names of individuals involved, description of the situation, choices for action considered, action that was taken, and the outcome of specific incidents in which one is involved. Recommended in instances of illness, injury, severe student misbehavior and emotionally volatile situations.

Anecdotal Summary
See Anecdotal Records

Authoritarian
Teaching style which demands immediate and unquestioning student obedience to teacher directives.

Blood Borne Pathogens
Bacteria, viruses, or other disease causing agents that can be carried and transmitted from one person to another via blood.

Bloom's Taxonomy
Six levels of thinking organized by Dr. Benjamin Bloom. The levels are organized from the lowest level of thinking to the highest in the following order: knowledge, comprehension, application, analysis, synthesis, and evaluation. These levels of thinking are often used as a basis for developing and presenting thought provoking questions to students.

Bodily Fluids
Term used for a number of fluids manufactured within the body. Usually used when referring to blood, semen, urine, and saliva.

Brainstorming
Teaching strategy to generate a lot of ideas in a short period of time. A prompt or topic is provided, then ideas are expressed freely and recorded within a given time limit. Evaluation of ideas is not a part of the brainstorming process. This strategy is often used as a springboard or starting point for other activities. (see also Dove Rules)

Captain (Cooperative Learning)
Cooperative learning student role of group leader responsible for keeping group members on-task and working towards the objective, sometimes also referred to as the Director or Manager.

Captivate and Redirect
Two step strategy for focusing the attention of a group of students. The first step involves capturing the students' attention by whispering, turning out the lights, clapping your hands, ringing a bell, etc. The second step is to immediately provide concise instructions that direct student attention to the desired activity. This strategy is often used at the beginning of class or when making a transition from one activity to the next.

Clean-up Captain (Cooperative Learning)
Cooperative Learning student role responsible for supervising the clean-up of the group's area at the end of the activity or project.

Coerce
See Coercive

Coercive
Interactions with students that attempt to achieve compliance to rules or instructions through the use of threats or force. Methods and practices intended to compel students to behave out of a fear of what will happen to them if they don't.

Common Sense Trap
Behavior management trap which involves trying to motivate students to comply with expectations by re-stating facts they already know, i.e. "If you don't get started, you're never going to get done." Usually unsuccessful, because students are not presented with any real incentive to change their behavior.

Concept Mapping
Strategy for organizing information about a central topic or theme. Key words and brief phrases are written down, circled, and connected to the main topic and each other by lines. Concept mapping can be used to introduce a topic, take notes, or summarize what students have learned. "Webbing" is another name for this strategy.

Confidentiality
Keeping personal information about students in confidence, i.e. not discussing student grades, disabilities, and/or behaviors with others, except on a need to know basis.

Consequences
A designated action or circumstance, either positive or negative, pre-determined to follow established student behavior. Example: A student completes their assignment, the consequence is they receive a sticker.

Consequential Behavior
Behavior which has significant impact on student learning or the classroom learning environment.

Cooperative Learning
Student learning strategy in which students work together in a small group (3-5 students) to complete a project or assignment. Typically each group member has a specific role or assignment and every member must contribute in order for the group to successfully complete the assigned task. Common student roles include captain, materials manager, recorder, procedure director, and clean-up captain.

Correct Individuals
Refers to the philosophy of changing the behavior of individual students by addressing and working with them one-on-one, rather than reprimanding or punishing an entire group of students for the inappropriate behavior of a single person.

Criticism Trap
Classroom management trap that involves criticizing students in an attempt to "shame" them into behaving appropriately. In reality the more students are criticized for a behavior the more likely the behavior is to continue because of the attention students are receiving. Criticism not only perpetuates inappropriate behaviors, but it also creates a negative classroom atmosphere.

Cultural Diversity
Similarities and differences of groups and/or individuals that align themselves with others based on common racial and/or ethnic characteristics or affiliations. Typical associations often include language, customs, and beliefs. (see also Ethnic Diversity and Racial Diversity)

Despair and Pleading Trap
Classroom management trap where a despondent teacher resorts to pleading with students to behave appropriately. This action communicates to students that the teacher doesn't know how to manage their behavior and that the classroom has pretty much been turned over to them. Rarely will students be compelled to behave appropriately in order to "help out" the teacher.

Disability
Term currently being used in place of handicap in reference to conditions experienced by individuals that result in the individual having special needs. (see also Disabled)

Disabled

An individual with disabilities such as mental retardation, hard of hearing, deafness, speech impaired, visually impaired, seriously emotionally disturbed, orthopedically impaired, or having other health impairments or learning disabilities such that they need special services or considerations.

DOVE Rules (of Brainstorming)

Rules and guidelines for conducting a brainstorming session.
D – Don't judge ideas, evaluation comes later.
O – Original and offbeat ideas are encouraged.
V – Volume of ideas, get as many possible in the time limit.
E – Everyone participates.

Due Care and Caution

The expected level of care and caution that an ordinarily reasonable and prudent person would exercise under the same or similar circumstances.

Early Finisher

Individual student leaning activity designated as appropriate for students to be engaged in when they finish an assignment or project earlier than the rest of the class, or prior to the beginning of the next class activity. Examples: crossword puzzles, silent reading, art projects, etc.

Echo the Correct Response (Questioning/ Risk-Free Environment)

Strategy used to generate a positive and risk-free classroom environment when a student responds incorrectly to a question. The incorrect response is acknowledged, then the question and the student's attention are directed to another student. Once a correct response has been given, the question is re-directed to the student who gave the incorrect response. The student can now "echo" the correct response and feel positive about their ability to answer the question.

Emergency Situations

An unexpected situation requiring prompt action to maintain or secure the safety and well being of students. Examples: fire, earthquake, bomb threat, flood, tornado, chemical spill, etc.

Ethnic Diversity

Similarities and differences between groups of people classified according to common traits, values, and heritage. Examples may include food, clothing, music and rituals. (see also Cultural Diversity and Racial Diversity)

Evacuation Map

A map designating the closest and alternative emergency exits, as well as the recommended route for reaching these exits, from a given location. Such a map should be posted in every classroom.

Evacuation Procedures

Specified actions to be taken in the event that students must leave the school building due to fire, or other emergency situations. Often such procedures include recognizing the evacuation signal, escorting students out of the building to a designated safe zone, and accounting for students once the evacuation has taken place.

Expectations

Established levels or standards of student behavior. Traditionally referred to as classroom rules.

Facilitator

One who enables or assists another in accomplishing a goal or objective, i.e. a teacher facilitates student learning by providing instruction, materials, and assistance as needed.

Field Trip

An educational activity in which students travel to a location other than the usual classroom or designated learning area. Often field trips involve the transportation of students to and from school grounds. Special legal considerations and supervision responsibilities are associated with student participation in field trip activities. (see also Permission Slips and Supervision)

Firm, Fair, and Friendly

Classroom management code of behavior which fosters a positive classroom atmosphere through firm, fair, and friendly teacher-to-student interactions.

Five-Minute Filler

A whole class learning activity that can be completed in approximately five minutes.

Usually teacher directed and often used to fill empty class time while waiting for the bell, lunch, recess, etc.

Frequency
The rate at which an event or action occurs and/or reoccurs. Example: A student leaving their seat to sharpen their pencil three times in twenty minutes.

Gifted and Talented
A student ability classification which indicates exceptional students who demonstrate above average ability, a high level of task commitment, and advanced creativity. These students often function at a higher intellectual level than their peers of the same age. Special programs are often instituted to provide advanced learning opportunities for such students.

Handicap
See Disability

Higher Level Questioning
Asking questions which require more than a recall of learned facts in response. Higher level questions require students to synthesize, summarize, classify, compare, apply, generalize, and/or evaluate known information before they answer the question.

Homework Assignments
Worksheets, projects, or other assignments which students are supposed to complete at home after school hours. Includes both the completion of assignments started in class and independent "at home" projects.

I Understand
Classroom management strategy used to acknowledge and stop student protests before redirecting the student's attention to appropriate on-task behavior, without becoming emotionally involved in the situation. Example: Student, "You are the worst teacher we've ever had." Teacher, "I understand. However as your teacher for today you are expected to follow my directions. Please open your science book to page 132 and begin silently reading the chapter."

IDEA
Individuals with Disabilities, Education Act – Public Law 94-142
Established in 1975 and originally called "The Education for All Handicapped Children Act," this law provides that all disabled children between the ages of 3 and 21 are entitled to free public education.

IEP
Individual Education Plan established for students with special leaning needs. The plan is developed by a team which includes the student, his/her parent(s), teachers, and professionals. It details the goals and objectives of educational services to be provided as well as listing the special and regular activities that the student will participate in.

Incentives
Student rewards that provide motivation for appropriate behavior. Examples: a fun activity after everyone finishes the assignment, a certificate recognizing student achievement, tickets for a drawing received for being on-task or working quietly, etc.

Inconsequential Behavior
Student behavior, that may or may not be annoying, which does not significantly detract from the learning environment or prevent students from achieving learning objectives and goals.

Instructive Language
Directions, expectations, or rules that instruct students regarding what they are supposed to do or how they are supposed to behave versus detailing what they are "not" supposed to do. Examples: work silently vs. no talking, walk down the hall vs. no running, quietly discuss this with your partner vs. don't talk too loud, etc.

Intrinsic (Motivation)
Motivation based upon an internal and personal reward such as a sense of satisfaction or pride in a job well done.

Intensity
Relating to the degree of concentration or effort required. Example: The intensity of completing a challenging math assignment is greater than listening to the teacher read a chapter from a book after lunch.

KWL
A learning strategy that begins by identifying what the learner knows about a topic and what

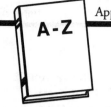

the learner wants to know about the topic. A teaching and/or learning experience then takes place and the activity concludes with the learner identifying what they have learned about the topic.

Learning Exercise

An activity, project, lesson or assignment implemented for the purpose of educating students.

Least Restrictive Environment

Regarding the education rights of students with disabilities, referring to their right be educated and treated in an environment and manner similar to their nondisabled peers. This often involves mainstreaming disabled students into regular classes and making individual accommodations as needed to serve these students in a "regular" classroom environment.

Lesson Plans

A detailed set of instructions which outline classroom activities for the day, including lessons to be taught, materials to be used, schedules to be met, and other pertinent information relating to student instruction and classroom management.

Mainstream

The enrollment of a disabled student in a regular education class, for the purpose of educating them in a least restrictive learning environment. Often involves individual adaptation of activities and assignments according to the specific needs of the student.

Materials Manager (Cooperative Learning)

Cooperative learning student role responsible for obtaining and returning equipment, materials, and supplies necessary for the activity.

Media Center

An updated term for the school library, as it is now offers access to information in a variety of ways including video tapes and computers in addition to traditional books and magazines.

Medication

Any substance, either over-the-counter or prescription, used to treat disease, injury or pain.

Monitor

To supervise or keep watch over student actions and behaviors.

Motivators

Consequences which inspire and encourage students to accomplish tasks or behave in an established manner. Motivators can either be tangible objects such as stickers, candy and certificates; special privileges such as being first in line, talk time, and fun activities; or recognition and acknowledgment of efforts through either verbal or nonverbal communication. (see also Rewards)

Negative Consequences

Undesirable actions or circumstances that are designated as a punishment when established standards for student behavior are not met. Example: A student brings a weapon to school, the weapon is confiscated and the student is expelled.

Negative Interactions

Any teacher/student interaction, either verbal or nonverbal, which is critical, derogatory, unfavorable, or accusatory in nature.

Neglect

A failure to provide a child under one's care with proper food, clothing, shelter, supervision, medical care, or emotional stability.

Noncoercive

Practices and methods that do not utilize force, pressure, criticism, fear, or other negative motivators to achieve desired student behavior.

Nonverbal (interactions)

Communication which does not involve speaking, i.e. smile of encouragement, written praise, disapproving look, etc.

Normal Voice

The tone and volume of voice one would use in everyday conversations with friends or family members.

Note Cards

A set of index cards (3x5 or 5x7) with one card designated for each school where you might be assigned to teach. On the card is listed the name of the school, school address, school telephone number, school start time, name of the principal and secretary, driving and parking directions, and approximate travel time.

Off-task
Not engaged in an assigned learning activity. Example: Student is writing a note when they are supposed to be completing a crossword puzzle.

On-task
To be actively and appropriately engaged in an assigned learning activity.

Operational (Expectations)
Expectations or rules for student behavior which define a student operation or action. Examples: keep your feet on the floor, follow directions the first time they are given, set your pencil on the desk, raise your hand for permission to speak, etc. (see also Instructive Language)

Pacing
The speed at which students are expected to complete an assignment or the rate at which a teacher moves from one activity to the next, in order to complete a designated number of activities in a specified amount of time.

Permission Slips
Document signed by the parent and/or legal guardian of a student authorizing permission for the student to participate in a specific activity, i.e. field trip. A signed permission slip must be received before a student can legally leave school property in conjunction with a learning experience.

Physical (Force)
The inappropriate use of one's body to compel a student to behave appropriately or in administering punishment for inappropriate behavior. Examples: hitting, shoving, lifting, spanking, slapping, kicking, etc.

Physical and Verbal Force Trap
Classroom management trap in which the teacher resorts to physical force or verbal threats and abuse to achieve desired student behavior. Not only are such actions inappropriate but in most situations they are also against the law.

Positive Interactions
A favorable action or communication between teacher and student which recognizes student effort or appropriate behavior. Example: A teacher makes a positive comment about how well a group of students is working together.

Positive Reinforcement
A positive interaction used to acknowledge and compliment appropriate student behavior for the purpose of encouraging the continuation of such behavior in the future. Example: A teacher verbally praises the class for working diligently and quietly on a writing assignment.

Praise
Positive teacher-to-student interactions that acknowledge and compliment students regarding their behavior or accomplishments. Example: Teacher, "It looks like you've put a lot of time and effort into this project, keep up the good work."

Preventative Measures
Actions or steps taken to avert the occurrence of inappropriate behavior, i.e. establishing expectations and engaging students in constructive learning experiences.

Proactive (Instruction)
Instructing students regarding their behavior using language which describes the specific actions or activities they should be engaged in. (see also Instructive Language)

Procedure Director (Cooperative Learning)
Cooperative learning student role responsible for reading instructions, explaining procedures, and making sure that the activity is completed correctly.

Professional Dress
Clean, neat, and appropriate clothing attire for the teaching situation. As a general rule, jeans, t-shirts, sandals and other casual clothing is not considered professional or appropriate for the classroom setting. You should always dress at least as professionally as your permanent teacher counterparts.

Prohibitive Language
Words or phrases that detail actions or activities which students are forbidden to participate in. Using prohibitive language in the classroom may

actually increase the occurrence of inappropriate student actions because it draws attention to these types of behaviors. Examples: don't run in the hall, quit tapping your pencil, stop being rude. (see also Instructive Language)

Proximity
The physical distance between student and teacher. Often used in classroom management, where close proximity or nearness to students encourages appropriate behavior and often stops inappropriate behaviors that are occurring.

Questioning (Teaching Strategy)
An instruction strategy that involves asking topic related questions, and eliciting student response. Successful and effective questioning involves the utilization of higher level questions, directing questions to a specific student, and allowing appropriate wait-time for student response.

Questioning Trap
Classroom management trap in which the teacher wastes time and is drawn off-task by asking a student questions whose answers provide information unnecessary for stopping inappropriate behavior or getting the student on-task.

Racial Diversity
Similarities and differences of groups of individuals with certain physical or genetic features. These features may include skin color, body type, and facial features. (see also Cultural Diversity and Ethnic Diversity)

Recorder (Cooperative Learning)
Cooperative learning student role responsible for recording information regarding the assignment, including writing down activity results and other information provided by group members.

Re-evaluate the Situation
To take an objective second look at classroom circumstances in an effort to determine if there are underlying reasons why students are unable to complete assignments or meet expectations.

Reinforce
To encourage a specific student behavior by providing rewards or attention when the behavior is exhibited.

Reinforce Expected Behaviors
To encourage students to continue to behave in an appropriate or expected manner by providing ongoing praise, rewards, or positive attention when they behave in accordance with expectations.

Removal, Identify, and Redirect
Strategy for dealing with inappropriate student behavior which involves removing the student from the immediate learning environment, acknowledging disapproval of the inappropriate behavior, and providing specific instructions and expectations for future behavior.

Restate (Expectations)
To repeat or explain again student behavior expectations or assignment completion instructions.

Review Technique
A strategy used to recap important events and items students need to remember from the instructional day. Examples: listing homework assignments on the board, brainstorming things learned during the class, having students construct a concept map of what they learned from a lesson, asking students to name the things they need to remember and bring to class the following day, etc.

Rewards
Praise, tokens, or a tangible items given to recognize student achievement, accomplishments, or attitudes.

Risk-free Classroom Environment
A classroom environment where students feel comfortable sharing appropriate ideas and opinions without fear of being ridiculed or criticized for incorrect or original responses.

Safe Schools (Policies)
Policies and/or practices adopted by a school district for the purpose of fostering a school environment that is safe, conducive to learning, and free from unnecessary disruptions.

Sarcasm Trap
Classroom management trap that involves making contemptuous or ironic remarks aimed at belittling students. Usually results in a negative classroom atmosphere and bad feelings between students and the teacher.

Seating Chart
A chart or diagram depicting the arrangement of desks in the classroom and listing the name of each student in reference to where they sit. A seating chart can be easily made using a file folder and small Post-it Notes®. Have each student write their name on a post-it note then arrange the notes on the folder to reflect where students sit.

Self-starter Activity
A simple project or assignment typically used at the beginning of the day or class period, which students can complete on their own without instructions or help from the teacher.

Sexual Harassment
Behavior that is unwanted or unwelcome, is sexual in nature or gender-based, is severe, pervasive and/or repeated, has an adverse impact on the workplace or academic environment, and often occurs in the context of a relationship where one person has more formal power than the other (i.e. supervisor/employee, or faculty/student).

Short Activity
Teacher directed lessons or activities that require 20 minutes to an hour to complete. Often implemented when the lesson plans left by the permanent teacher are unable to be carried out or there is a significant amount of extra class time.

Special Duties
Extra teacher responsibilities or assignments in addition to usual classroom teaching activities. Examples: bus duty, hall monitor, cafeteria supervisor, playground duty.

State the Facts
A direct and to the point classroom management technique that involves clearly and concisely stating student behavior expectations and consequences if the expectations are not met, then immediately instructing students to engage in an assigned task. Appropriate for situations when students are testing the limits, willfully being off-task or making excuses for inappropriate behavior.

Step-by-step Process (Transitions)
Providing a clear course of action for students to make the transition from one activity to the next.

The process involves instruction regarding, what to do about the activity they are currently engaged in, what to do with the materials they are using, what new materials they will need, what to do with these new materials, and how much time they have to make the transition. Example: "You have one minute to finish your science crossword, put it in your desk, take out your silent reading book, and start reading. Please begin."

Stop and Re-direct
A classroom management strategy for dealing with inappropriate student behavior. It involves instructing the student to stop the behavior they are currently engaged in and re-directing their actions through further instructions as to what they should be doing. Example: "Jason, please stop wandering around the room. Sit down at your desk and spend the rest of the class period working on your homework assignment."

Substitute Teacher Report
A report written by a substitute teacher and left for the permanent teacher. It outlines the activities of the day, explains any deviation from the lesson plans, and notes student behavior (including inappropriate behavior the permanent teacher needs to be aware of and information about students who were particularly helpful).

Super SubPack
A box, bag, briefcase, or backpack filled with teaching resource materials including personal and professional items, classroom supplies, student rewards and motivators, and activity materials, which a substitute teacher assembles and brings to teaching assignments.

Supervision (of Students)
To oversee all of the activities and actions of students in one's charge at all times and in all settings and circumstances (i.e. field trips, field trip transportation, recess, assemblies, evacuations).

Threat Trap
A classroom management trap that involves the teacher verbalizing drastic, highly undesirable, and often unrealistic consequences if student do not behave appropriately. The premise of making threats is that students will fear the consequences so much that they don't dare behave inappropriately. Most threats are issued

out of frustration and the teacher often loses credibility when students do behave inappropriately because the teacher does not really want to, or can not, enforce the threatening consequences they have established.

Transitioning
The act or process of changing from one activity, topic of study, or assignment to another. (see also Step-by-step Process)

Traps
Classroom management scenarios (7) in which the teacher becomes "trapped" due to poor or improper choices in dealing with student behaviors. Once in a trap the teacher loses some of their ability and authority to direct student actions. (see also Criticism Trap, Common Sense Trap, Questioning Trap, Despair and Pleading Trap, Threat Trap, Physical and Verbal Force Trap)

Verbal Interactions
Communication or other interactions involving speaking.

Verbal Force
The inappropriate use of language, threats, tone or intensity of voice to compel a student to behave appropriately.

Verbal Recognition
The use of spoken word to praise and/or acknowledge student effort, progress or accomplishments.

Wait Time
The elapsed time or pause between when a question is asked and a response is expected. A recommended wait time is 5-10 seconds. This allows students time to formulate an answer and verbalize a response.

Warm-up/Starter Activity
An introductory activity used at the beginning of a lesson or assignment to engage students, channel their thoughts, or prepare students to achieve the lesson objective.

Whisper
Classroom management strategy in which the

teacher uses a very quiet voice to communicate instructions and get the attention of the entire class, rather than speaking loudly or shouting to be heard over the classroom noise level.

Work Together
Students working together to accomplish a task or complete an assignment. (see also Cooperative Learning).

To learn more about Substitute Teaching:

visit us on the internet

at http://subed.usu.edu

or call us at 1-800-922-4693

Substitute Teaching Institute
Utah State University
6516 Old Main Hill
Logan, UT
84322-6516

Substitute Professional
Reference Guide

*Substitute Teacher Handbook: Secondary for Grades 9-12, ISBN 1890563102, Substitute Teaching Institute, Utah State University, 1999.

*SubInstructor, Interactive computer CD for use with the Substitute Teacher Handbooks. Substitute Teaching Institute, Utah State University, 2000.

*SubOrientation Video, An introduction to the world of substitute teaching. Substitute Teaching Institute, Utah State University, 1999.

*Classroom Management: 5 Skills Every Substitute Teacher Should Have, 3 hour audio presentation by Dr. Glenn Latham. Substitute Teaching Institute, Utah State University, 1998.

*Available From The Substitute Teaching Institute, Utah State University, 6516 Old Main Hill, Logan, UT 84322-6516, 1-800-922-4693

Mastering the Art of Substitute Teaching, S. Harold Collins, 1995. ISBN 0931993024, Garlic Press.

Classroom Management for Substitute Teachers, S. Harold Collins, 1982. ISBN 0931993032, Garlic Press.

Instant Success for Classroom Teachers, New and Substitute Teachers, Barbara Cawthorne, 1981. ISBN 0960666605, Greenfield Publications.

The First Days of School, How to be an Effective Teacher, Harry K. Wong & Rosemary Tripi Wong, 1998. ISBN 0962936006, Harry K. Wong Publications.

Substitute Teaching: A Handbook for Hassle-Free Subbing, Barbara Pronin, 1983. ISBN 0312774842, St. Martin's Press.

Super Sub: A Must-Have Handbook for Substitute Teachers, Cary Seeman & Shannon Hofstrand, 1998. ISBN 0673363805, Goodyear Pub Co.

A Handbook for Substitute Teachers, Anne Wescott Dodd, 1989. ISBN 0398060975, Charles C Thomas Pub Ltd.

Sub Survival: A Handbook for the Substitute Elementary Teacher, Danna Downing & Fritz J. Erickson, 1996. ISBN 1556911254, Learning Publications.

Substitute Teaching: Planning for Success, Elizabeth Manera, Marji Gold-Vukson & Jennifer Kapp, 1996. ISBN 0912099062, Kappa Delta Pi Publications.

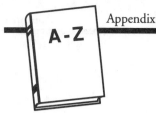

Classroom and Behavior

Management Books

<u>Coercion and its Fallout</u>, Murray Sidman, 1989. Authors Cooperative, Inc., Publishers, P.O. Box 53, Boston, MA 02199, ISBN 0962331120

<u>The Teacher's Encyclopedia of Behavior Management, 100 Problems/500 Plans, *for grades K-9*</u>, Randall S. Sprick and Lisa M. Howard, 1995. Sopris West, 1140 Boston Avenue, Longmont, CO 80501, ISBN 1570350310

<u>Bringing Out the Best in People</u>, *How to Apply the Astonishing Power of Positive Reinforcement*, Aubrey C. Daniels, 1994, 208 pages. McGraw-Hill, Inc., ISBN 0070153582

<u>The Acting-Out Child</u>, *Coping with Classroom Disruption*, Hill M .Walker, 1995, 420 pages. Sopris West, 1140 Boston Avenue, Longmont, CO 80501, ISBN 1570350477

<u>Antisocial Behavior in School: Strategies and Best Practices</u>, Hill M. Walker, Geoff Colvin, Elizabeth Ramsey, 1995, 481 pages.   Brooks/Cole Publishing Company, A division of International Thomson Publishing Inc., ISBN 0534256449

<u>Talented But Troubled</u>, *Reclaiming Children and Youth*, Journal of Emotional and Behavioral Problems, Vol. 6, No. 4 Winter 1998, Pro-Ed Journals, 8700 Shoal Creek Blvd., Austin, TX 78757-6897

School Supply Companies

Cuisenaire 1-800-237-3142 to request a current catalog. K-9 materials for Mathematics and Science

Delta Education   1-800-442-5444   to request a current catalog.   Hands-On Math activity books and supplies; Hands-On Science activity books and supplies

Nasco   1-800-558-9595 to request a current catalog.   Health, Arts & Crafts, Math, Science, Language Arts, Social Studies, and Music Materials

Summit Learning 1-800-777-8817   to request a current catalog. K-9 Math, Language Arts, Science; Early Childhood

Education Activity Books

Read It With Bookmarks, Barbara L. Goldenhersh, 1992. ISBN 1882429079, Substitute Teaching Institute, Utah State University.

Substitute Ingredients, Grades 3-8, S. Harold Collins, 1974. ISBN 0931993016, Garlic Press.

Substitute Teacher's Reference Manual, Carol A. Jones, 1998. ISBN 088280135X, Etc Publications.

Substitute Teacher's Handbook Activities and Projects, Mary F. Redwine, 1970. ISBN 822466007, Lake Pub Co.

Teacher (Substitute) Survival Activities Kit Vol. 1, Thomas J. Randquist, 1998. ISBN 1884239218, Nova Media Incorporated.

At Your Local Bookstore

Monster Mad Libs, Roger Price & Leonard Stern, ISBN 0843100583. Commercial version of the Silly Stories found in this handbook.

I SPY, Walter Wick & Jean Marzollo, ISBN 0590450875.   A picture book of riddles.

The Mammoth Book of Fun and Games, Richard B. Manchester, ISBN 0884860442. Over 400 games, jokes, and puzzles.

The Giant Book of Games, Will Shortz, ISBN 081291951. Games and puzzles compiled from Games magazine.

Kids' Giant Book of Games, Karen C. Anderson, ISBN 0-12921992. Games and puzzles compiled from Games magazine.

Word Games For Kids, Robert Allen. ISBN 1559585935. Word puzzles for kids divided into four levels of difficulty.

Brain Bafflers, Robert Steinwachs, ISBN 0806987871.

Puzzles Perplexities & Obfuscations, George Hardy, ISBN 0806982101.

More Two Minute Mysteries, Donald J. Sobol, ISBN 0590447882. Over 60 mysteries to read and solve in two minutes or less.

More 5 Minute Mysteries, Ken Weber, ISBN 156138058X. Mysteries to read and solve in five minutes or less.

1000 Crazy Jokes For Kids, Ballantine Books, ISBN 0345346947. Jokes for children of all ages.

Smart Alec's Knock Knock Jokes For Kids, Ballantine Books, ISBN 0-345-35196-7. Knock Knock jokes kids love.

Recommended Children's Books

Alexander and the Terrible, Horrible, No Good, Very Bad Day	Judith Viorst
Amelia Bedelia	Peggy Parrish
Animals Should Definitely Not Wear Clothing	Ron Barrett
Anansi and the Moss-Covered Rock	Eric Kimmel
Brown Bear, Brown Bear, What Do You See?	Bill Martin Jr.
Cloudy With a Chance of Meat Balls	Judi Barrett
The Day Jimmy's Boa Ate the Wash	Trinka H. Noble
George and Martha	James Marshall
Giraffe and a Half	Shel Silverstein
Grandfather Tang's Story	Lee Tompert
Harold and the Purple Crayon	Crockett Johnson
Henny Penny	Paul Galdone
Horton Hatches the Egg	Dr. Seuss
If You Give a Mouse a Cookie	Laura J. Numeroff
It Could Always Be Worse	retold by Margot Zemoch
Koala Lou	Mem Fox
Lily's Purple Plastic Purse	Kevin Henkes
Lyle, Lyle, Crocodile	Bernard Waber
Mike Mulligan and His Steam Shovel	Virginia L. Burton
Miss Nelson is Missing	Harry Allard & James Marshall
The Napping House	Audrey Wood
Not in the House, Newton!	Judith Gilliland
Pinkerton, Behave!	Steven Kellogg
The Principal's New Clothes	Stephanie Calmenson
Slugs	David Greenburg
The Stinky Cheese Man	Jon Scieszka
Stone Soup	retold by Marcia Brown
Swamp Angel	Anne Isaacs
Sylvester and the Magic Pebble	William Steig
There's a Nightmare in My Closet	Mercer Mayer
The True Story of the Three Little Pigs	John Scieszka
The Very Hungry Caterpillar	Eric Carle
Where the Sidewalk Ends	Shel Silverstein
Where the Wild Things Are	Maurice Sendak
Z Was Zapped	Chris Van Allsburg

Where to Get Books

Many of these popular titles can be found on the shelves of local bookstores. If they are not already in stock, any of these books can be special ordered by providing the sales associate with the title and author. For inexpensive books look at second-hand bookstores, or check with a teacher to see if they, or their students, receive book order forms directly from school publishing companies. For a great selection of books you can use for free, visit your local library.

Substitute Teacher Report

Substitute: _____   Date: _____

Phone Number: _____   Grade/Class: _____

Substituted for: _____   School: _____

Notes regarding lesson plans:

I also taught:

Notes regarding behavior:

Terrific helpers:

Students who were absent:

Messages for the permanent teacher:

© Substitute Teaching Institute/Utah State University

A-Z

Teaching Journal

Date:	School:	Grade:	Who's class:	Notes:

Teaching Journal

Date: School: Grade: Who's class: Notes:

SubSurvey
Your Feedback is Valuable!

Substitute Teaching Institute
Utah State University

1. Previous years of substitute teaching experience: ❑ 0   ❑ 1   ❑ 2-3   ❑ 4+

2. Why are you a substitute teacher?

   Seeking a permanent teaching position?   ❑ Yes   ❑ No

   Enjoying temporary/part-time employment?   ❑ Yes   ❑ No

   Other _____

3. How long do you anticipate working as a substitute teacher?
   ❑ 1 month-1 year   ❑ 2-3 years   ❑ 4+ years

4. Please identify the usefulness of each chapter in the handbook. Rate each from not very useful (1) to very useful (5).

   1 2 3 4 5 The Professional Substitute Teacher (Chapter 1)

   1 2 3 4 5 Classroom Management (Chapter 2)

   1 2 3 4 5 Other Stuff You Should Know (Chapter 3)

   1 2 3 4 5 Teaching Strategies, Skills, and Suggestions (Chapter 4)

   1 2 3 4 5 Fill-In Activities (Chapter 5)

5. Which chapters in this book do you feel will be **most** beneficial to you as a substitute teacher? Explain why.

6. Which chapters in this book do you feel will be **least** beneficial to you as a substitute teacher? Explain why.

7. What changes would you make to the handbook?

Fax to: 435-797-2355 Mail to: 6516 Old Main Hill • Logan UT 84322-6516 • http://subed.usu.edu

SubInstructor CD
Interactive Substitute Teacher Training CD

Think of it as

"the best of"

four years of college

on CD.

A true innovation in the training of substitute teachers, the SubInstructor is a multimedia CD-Rom enabling substitute teachers to learn at their own pace without the time and cost commitment normal workshops require. Substitute teachers can view and review video clips and commentary of master teachers as they demonstrate specific skills and techniques for classroom management and instruction.

This SubInstructor CD will make a comprehensive training opportunity available to any substitute teacher with computer access. Designed to complement the Substitute Teacher Handbooks, it demonstrates and explains key aspects of being prepared and professional, classroom management, legal and education issues, teaching strategies, and fill-in activities. The interactive assessment component is an added benefit to the CD that allows users to review key concepts and test their knowledge. Estimated initial training time is between two and four hours depending on the experience level of the substitute teacher.

For more information contact your district SubOffice or log on to http://subed.usu.edu.

Skills are

the Essence of

Competence.

Begin your

training today!

SubInstructor
Substitute Training CD

UtahState
UNIVERSITY

Substitute Success Kit

Substitute Teacher Handbooks (K-8) or (9-12)

Hundreds of pages of practical expectations, classroom management skills, teaching strategies, and fill-in activities. The most widely used substitute teacher handbook in education today!

SubInstructor: An Interactive Substitute Teacher Training CD

See classroom management, teaching strategies, and fill-in activities used in the classroom. You'll see first hand how it's done, as well as be able to review it again, and again.

iSubAssociation Membership

You'll share e-mails from experts in the field of substitute teaching, as well as substitutes from across the country. You can download daily lesson plans, classroom management tips, and fill-in lesson plans. iSubAssociation provides support for increasing substitute teacher competency in the classroom. A must for every substitute teacher!

SubDiploma from the Substitute Teaching Institute

For the first time ever, you can receive a Substitute Teaching Diploma from the experts at Utah State University. Study the material and complete an on-line assessment and receive your SubDiploma! You'll not only benefit in skills and confidence, but recognition from your district.

For Less Than a Day's Pay, Receive the Most Comprehensive Success Tools Available!

– – – – – – – – – Substitute Order Form – – – – – – – – –

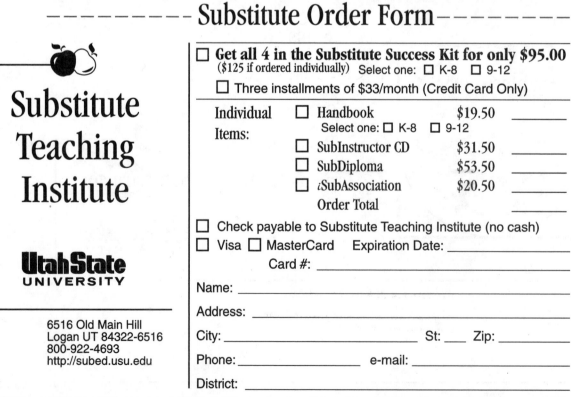

Substitute Teaching Institute

UtahState UNIVERSITY

6516 Old Main Hill
Logan UT 84322-6516
800-922-4693
http://subed.usu.edu

☐ **Get all 4 in the Substitute Success Kit for only $95.00**
($125 if ordered individually) Select one: ☐ K-8 ☐ 9-12
☐ Three installments of $33/month (Credit Card Only)

Individual Items:			
	☐ Handbook Select one: ☐ K-8 ☐ 9-12	$19.50	_____
	☐ SubInstructor CD	$31.50	_____
	☐ SubDiploma	$53.50	_____
	☐ iSubAssociation	$20.50	_____
	Order Total		_____

☐ Check payable to Substitute Teaching Institute (no cash)
☐ Visa ☐ MasterCard   Expiration Date: _____
       Card #: _____

Name: _____

Address: _____

City: _____ St: ___ Zip: _____

Phone: _____ e-mail: _____

District: _____